Find Your True

Find Your True Voice

*Stop Listening to Your Inner Critic, Heal
Your Trauma and Live a Life Full of Joy*

EMMY BRUNNER

PENGUIN LIFE

AN IMPRINT OF

PENGUIN BOOKS

PENGUIN LIFE

UK | USA | Canada | Ireland | Australia
India | New Zealand | South Africa

Penguin Life is part of the Penguin Random House group of companies
whose addresses can be found at global.penguinrandomhouse.com.

First published 2021
001

Copyright © Emmy Brunner, 2021

The moral right of the author has been asserted

The publisher is grateful for permission to quote on page 202 lyrics from:
'Baby We'll Be Fine' Words & Music by Matthew Berninger & Aaron Dessner © Copyright 2006
Val Jester Music. BMG Rights Management (US) LLC. All Rights Reserved. International
Copyright Secured. Used by permission of Hal Leonard Europe Limited.

Set in 13.5/16pt Garamond MT Std
Typeset by Jouve (UK), Milton Keynes
Printed and bound in Great Britain by Clays Ltd, Elcograf S.p.A.

The authorized representative in the EEA is Penguin Random House Ireland,
Morrison Chambers, 32 Nassau Street, Dublin D02 YH68

A CIP catalogue record for this book is available from the British Library

ISBN: 978—0—241—47453—2

www.greenpenguin.co.uk

For anyone trying to heal a wounded
heart . . . this is for you.

Thanks to Tuppence Middleton, who read these pages
before anyone else and whose help was invaluable.

To my girls Dixie and River,
you make my world so joyful.

And finally . . . T-Bone, the kindest man I have
ever known. Thank you for loving me so much.

Contents

CONTENTS

Time to Make a Start

It was May 2006 and I was wandering around a building looking for Room 342. As a newly qualified psychotherapist, I was visiting an organization called the Caron Foundation, an inpatient rehabilitation unit in Pennsylvania, in the United States. I was nervous, and keen to hide that fact. At the time I was working for a UK rehab that had sent me here to learn about Caron's processes, to see if they could teach us something.

I saw Room 342, knocked and pushed the door open, and introduced myself.

A petite woman with a warm smile welcomed me into the room. 'Hey, Emmy. Sit down. I'm going to tell you how we work and how we admit new clients, but first I want to tell you my story.'

What was this? Why was this woman being weird and telling me she was going to be sharing her story? I'm British, and it's in my DNA to find random acts of intimacy odd and uncomfortable. Not only that, but my own upbringing meant that I rejected any kind of vulnerability and had built a small fort around myself when it came to real connection with others.

I managed to mumble an obviously uncomfortable response, and she continued.

'Emmy, I want you to know that I see you. Now, I know

you're here to do a job and we'll get to that, but when someone shows up in my life I ask myself why they are here and
what the purpose of us meeting is. I'm going to tell you a
little bit about myself and my life, and I hope that it will
help you on your path.'

I asked her how she knew I needed help. How had I
given away so much in such a small amount of time and
in so few words?

'I don't know for certain, but you're a young woman
working in a job committed to helping others in pain.
In my world, that usually means that we've known great
pain ourselves, or that we are still in pain and looking for
a way out. Either way, I think I have something to offer.'

And so I sat and I listened.

The woman told me that the Caron Foundation had
saved her life many years ago – before that, she genuinely
could not have imagined a life where she could be happy
or experience true joy. She explained that she had learned
how to turn towards her pain, rather than repressing or
smothering it, and how connecting and sharing with
others had changed everything for her.

It was as though a lightbulb switched on for the first
time, and everything I'd struggled to see about myself was
suddenly absolutely clear. Over the coming months I realized that if I wanted my life to change, I would have to
grieve my past and heal the wounds that I was carrying
around. I came to understand that what I can now identify as my own 'unwell' behaviours and 'problems' were
responses and survival strategies I'd developed to cope
with past trauma.

In subsequently processing that trauma, I learned and developed a set of coping tools that allowed me to foster a compassionate relationship with myself. This gave me the courage and confidence to pursue the life I really wanted. I became able to embrace intimacy and vulnerability in relationships, pursue my career ambitions with confidence and focus, and develop a sense of self-care that remains my anchor today.

I want to take the opportunity to show you how to do the same. I have written this book to share with you the lessons that I have learned about healing, honesty, recovery and kindness. I will show you how to begin to heal your own wounds, establish a compassionate relationship with yourself, and empower yourself to live the life that you really want. Together, we will look at understanding why and how things came to be, and I will show you how you can develop practical tools to cope.

I mentioned that my problems, as I saw them then, were rooted in trauma. When I use this word you may imagine a whole multitude of experiences that could have caused me this psychological harm.

The word 'trauma' is often the first obstacle that we have to overcome when we begin the work, because it means such different things to different people. Many of my clients do not see the experiences that have led them to my door as particularly traumatic. If you also feel this way, let me ask if you are able to identify with any of the following questions:

Do you find yourself pursuing relationships with people who are not available to you?

Do you struggle with your body image – constantly feeling like you don't look good enough?

Do you find yourself plagued by anxiety or depression?

Do you frequently talk to or think about yourself in a punishing, critical way?

Do you often feel lost, hopeless and ashamed, and use sex, food, alcohol, drugs or relationships as a tool to harm yourself?

Do you feel like your behaviours around food are prohibiting you from living a full and courageous life?

Do you often feel stuck in a destructive and toxic pattern or cycle?

Do you yearn for a way out of this cycle, often wishing your life could be simpler, happier and more stable, but also fear the way out too?

If you relate to any of these questions, the likelihood is that something traumatic has happened in your life that has affected the way you see the world and act within it. You might not always be able to pinpoint where and when that hurt happened – it might be something that feels relatively small and which you've previously overlooked – but this process will help you to identify your wounds and begin the process of healing.

If any – or all – of these questions apply to you (or someone you love), then what you're going through is really tough. Living in a cycle where you are either ambivalent about life or engaged in destructive behaviours is exhausting, confusing, frightening and lonely. It is a pervasive kind of feeling that affects health, wellbeing, work, relationships, finances and confidence.

But you don't have to live this way. Really – things can change. In fact, they can transform. You *can* move beyond this way of existing and learn to love who you really are. There *is* a freer and more meaningful future out there waiting. All you need to do is to take that first step.

How do I know? Because I've done it, and I've helped others do it countless times. I have been a clinician for over fifteen years, working with trauma and low self-esteem, but I've been a fellow sufferer for even longer. I know the pain of living with an all-consuming critical voice in my head, and feeling paralysed and stuck. I'm also someone who broke her way free of it, and wants to show you how you can too.

Recovery has given me the opportunity to heal, and also a wealth of life-enhancing relationships. As painful as some of my experiences have been, I can now recognize their value and empathize more deeply with others who are walking a similar path. From years of running therapy groups, I have come to see how mutual sharing and connection act as a catalyst for positive change.

I often tell the following anecdote at the beginning of therapy groups. It's one that reflects the impact we can have when we support each other:

A woman is walking down a street and falls into a hole. The walls are so steep that she is stuck and can't get out.

She shouts up to the street to ask for help and a doctor looks down. He throws down a prescription and walks away.

She shouts for help again and a holy man looks down. The holy man writes down a prayer and then throws it into the hole and walks away.

She shouts again and this time a friend looks down. The friend jumps down into the hole with her.

'Are you crazy?' she asks her friend. 'Now we're both stuck in this hole!'

'Yes, I know!' the friend responds. 'But I've been down here before and I know the way out.'

I too *know the way out*. That's why I'm writing this book. It contains information about my clinical approach – how and why it works – as well as stories from people I've worked with. There are also some workbook sections called Recovery Tools, where you'll be asked to answer questions and make notes in order to help you better understand how to start healing. Be sure to take it all at your own pace and be as honest as you can.

We are going to explore what the 'unwell voice' is, where it's come from and how it limits you. I will show you how to strengthen and empower yourself, and finally how to fully realize your own potential so that you can be free to live the life that you've always wanted.

Please take things slowly, and don't stress if things feel a little overwhelming or don't fully resonate straight away – that's totally normal, and during my own healing I had to revisit things several times before I was truly able to absorb and benefit from them. Feel free to stop at any point and come back to that chapter later if that feels right for you. I've worked to create a process that allows you to evolve and grow along the way, but I want you to give yourself permission to dictate the pace and always try to begin each step with an open heart and mind.

With love, faith and compassion for you and your healing journey,

Emmy x

Step 1: Identify Your Internal Voices

So many of us learn to keep parts of ourselves hidden;
we are never really seen by others, and thus
we are left feeling hollow and lonely.

**As we begin this journey together, we're going to look
at identifying where the 'work' might be for us. We're
going to start exploring any destructive or dysfunctional patterns that might have become established,
and consider what the 'internal narrative' might be
that is driving our decisions and responses to things.
Don't worry if it feels odd to consider yourself having destructive patterns. My experience is that it is
incredibly helpful to gain insight into what is driving
our decisions – because when we do, we realize that
we're more powerful in dictating the course of our
lives than we perhaps previously thought.**

The big question: Am I stuck in a destructive pattern?

During the early years of my career as a clinician, I worked
to help those suffering with mental health issues to find
recovery. I began to realize that the 'wounds' I saw in those
suffering with eating disorders were the same as those I

encountered in those suffering with anxiety, or depression, or a personality disorder, or addiction. I recognized that existing treatment models failed to connect to the 'heart' of the sufferer, and came to firmly believe that recovery from an eating disorder was about so much more than weight restoration or a stabilization of food behaviours. It was all tethered to a chronic sense of self-loathing, and the 'symptoms' that they were struggling with were simply the destructive tools they had developed to try to cope with life.

Over the years I came to notice that, although my attention had fallen on those in personal crises and those whose symptoms had become unsustainable – their weight too low, their addiction too chronic, the personal fallout too big – actually there was pain all around me, in all of us, including those of us who were managing to function and hold down relationships and jobs. We weren't descending into a crisis, but we were deeply wounded nonetheless. Our pain was perhaps less evident, but there was no doubt that it was there.

I started to investigate further, speaking to colleagues, friends and relatives. So many of the people I spoke to shared that they felt unworthy of seeking help or treatment – they did not see themselves as 'unwell'. They struggled to articulate what it was that they needed help for; they just had a pervasive feeling that something wasn't right and that they were 'failing'. They all approached life as something that they were trying to 'get through' from one day to the next – it wasn't something that they approached with a full and joyful heart.

In the cases where people were able to recognize that they were struggling with something tangible – for example, anxiety, depression or issues with food – many of these people also felt confused, because when they had sought help from their GP or other healthcare professionals, they'd either been told there was nothing wrong with them or that they were not physically sick enough to access help. I myself related to this pattern so acutely – when our pain is not seen or validated by those around us, we start to believe that *we* are the problem.

One of the things that united all of these people that I spoke to – and something I was able to identify within myself – was the presence of something that I call the 'unwell voice'.

The unwell voice is something that exists internally. It is spiteful, unkind and seeks to undermine all that we are and do. It criticizes us for how we look, sound and behave. It undermines our achievements, sabotages our

enjoyment of experiences and consistently leaves us feeling inadequate.

If you've picked up this book and read this far, I'm guessing that you too know this voice?

Your unwell voice

It is the unwell voice that persuades us that we are not worthy of support and that we are the problem. It encourages us to isolate ourselves and to hide huge parts of ourselves from others, because this voice is fuelled by fear and shame. It convinces us that if people knew who we *really* were, then we would be rejected. As a result, we are never truly seen by others, and thus we are left feeling hollow and lonely.

I know for certain that when I look back on the loneliest times of my life, they were when I had abandoned myself and I wasn't acknowledging my pain. I functioned, showed up and took part, but I didn't allow anyone 'in'. I could be abrupt and defensive, and found any form of intimacy impossible. I can see now that it was the unwell voice that drove these strategies for defence against vulnerability.

The unwell voice is almost always created in childhood, and is formed from the messages we receive and the experiences we've had. It develops as an attempt to protect us from our reality, and creates a set of core beliefs to help us cope with the environment within which we are being raised. It reinforces behaviours and beliefs in order to try to secure whatever love is available, and ultimately denies our own needs as we become conditioned to adapt and change in order to pursue that affection; for example, *My father doesn't give me any attention or affection so I will strive to do well in school/work in ways that are recognized by him, to try to garner his praise.*

The unwell voice's core belief system is:

- *I am unlovable/unworthy/undeserving/not good enough.*
- *I compare myself with others to reinforce my sense of unworthiness and inferiority.*
- *I am a victim of other people's choices and behaviours. My life cannot change until other people change.*
- *Things are good or bad; right or wrong.*

Being able to identify with this voice can be painful, but it's in the knowing that we start to become empowered. For myself, it was a real shock to come to terms with the fact that my life choices had been dictated by an unwell voice and that I had been in the pattern of some very destructive behaviours for a long time – from pushing away people I loved to repeatedly seeking out abusive relationships. I realized that if I wanted things to change, then something within myself had to shift.

As difficult as it was to accept this truth, in doing so I was able to face myself and give myself the opportunity to change how the rest of my life was going to play out. I made a commitment to show up and be honest with myself about my self-destructive tendencies, because

I realized that the more I avoided them, the more they would consume me.

The journey of healing is one that we can go on together. It takes patience, compassion and a willingness to explore new ideas. It involves creating space to observe patterns in our own lives, but by doing so we will be able to develop a deeper self-awareness.

The unwell voice is constantly judging and assessing our actions in every area of our lives, undermining our self-esteem and confidence. This hostile voice deters us from making positive changes in our lives, and creates an increased sense of distrust of ourselves and our own judgements. The unwell voice might be telling us things like:

- 'You're fat.'
- 'You shouldn't apply for that job because you don't stand a chance.'
- 'You shouldn't speak, you'll just sound stupid.'
- 'You're weird.'
- 'You're unlovable.'

This voice can get very loud and overwhelming, and many of us can end up just living in a state of reacting to and trying to placate the unwell voice – but allowing the unwell voice to frame our view of the world leads to self-limiting behaviours and negative consequences.

Everyone hears the unwell voice in slightly different ways, but when we break it down into its simplest form it basically looks like this: *self-critical thought = self-harming behaviour.*

For example:

- *I'm fat* = restricting food intake
- *I have nothing to say* = social isolation
- *I'm not capable* = playing small in your career

Be aware too that, while the unwell voice is frequently spiteful and cruel, it can also adopt a soothing guise. For example, it might whisper, 'Don't go out tonight – you're tired, and seeing those friends will only make you feel bad.' This seemingly kind tone hides a deeper desire to isolate you and hurt you. That's why it's important to follow these thoughts through: if you don't see your friends, what will the likely outcome be? One possibility is that the unwell voice will then attack you anyway ('You're such a loser, you couldn't even go and see your friends, now they're all going to hate you'). The other possibility is that you'll miss out on the laughter, chats and connection with friends that make life so worthwhile.

Essentially, the unwell voice draws strength every time we are unkind to ourselves. The unwell voice's purpose is to:

- Strengthen a sense of self that is built upon what other people have told us about ourselves and external experiences we have had.
- Protect us from painful events in our past.
- Keep us in familiar patterns because this is what feels safe.
- Reinforce feelings and thoughts we've had since childhood.

- Seek out people and experiences that reinforce the unconscious beliefs that we have about ourselves and the world.
- Serve as a tool to prevent our inner child from acknowledging anything that feels too painful.

Be mindful at this stage that your unwell voice will be raging against this material, because it will feel very threatening. It will feel angry and out of control when it is challenged, and this can shift a person into feeling defended and attacked.

If you are able to recognize these feelings being triggered within yourself, try to take a step back, make a

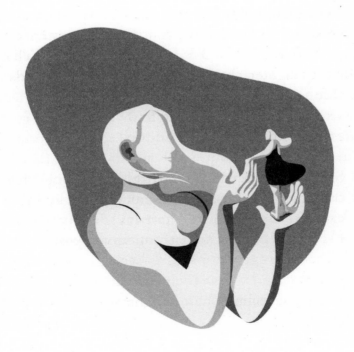

commitment to becoming a loving witness to your own experiences, and make a choice to continue your pursuit of truth.

Your well voice

Conversely, we also have an internal 'well voice'. Any voice we hear that comes from a place of kindness, that is telling us things will be okay or is encouraging us to seek support . . . that's our well voice. Some people like to think of it as a kind of wise woman within themselves, or a guide who lets them know when something isn't feeling right or if anything needs to change.

For some, the well voice can be heard quite clearly, but for most of us it's just a whisper – it needs encouragement to speak up and be heard. Every person that I've ever met has a well voice inside, however quiet it is at first. It's something compassionate and nurturing that lives within us – it's probably the voice that told you to reach for this book, for instance.

I'm going to help you cultivate and strengthen your well voice, whether you can hear it yet or not. This process can take a little patience, though. When you're so familiar with listening to a critical, destructive voice, trying to connect with something more positive can be pretty challenging.

When my clients hear their unwell voice, I ask them how a more compassionate voice might respond. Very quickly, they reply, 'I don't know.' So then I ask them how they'd respond to a friend, and suddenly they begin to flourish, coming up with numerous compassionate and kind responses in just a minute. This is a good way to kick-start the development of your well voice: in response to any self-critical thoughts that pop up, imagine you're talking to a good friend or anybody you love. After all, this process is about nurturing a kinder relationship with yourself.

As time goes on, you'll get better at differentiating between your well and unwell voices. It can feel a little laborious early on but it gets easier, trust me. By challenging your shameful feelings about yourself and focusing on what you want instead of what you don't want, you'll start feeling stronger. And as you become better able to recognize or predict how the unwell voice will respond to certain situations and scenarios, you'll be better able to prepare a response from your well voice. If at any point you find your unwell voice gets really angry, then it's probably feeling threatened. Well done — this means you're on the right track!

Get to know your voices better

The journey of self-healing is all about acknowledging the presence of both an unwell and a well voice inside your head, and starting to strengthen the well voice until it becomes masterful, directing your thoughts and actions. This book is a guide to help you become empowered, allowing your choices to be governed by a confidence about what feels 'right' for you, as opposed to your fears and your perceived limitations.

I know it may seem impossible to imagine a time when you think and feel differently from how you do today, but I'm here to tell you that it's not. After all, you weren't born thinking and feeling this way about yourself. This journey is an opportunity to rekindle – or discover for the first time – a relationship with yourself that is grounded in compassion.

Your unwell behaviours and struggles to be vulnerable are evidence that you are hurting. The more we become familiar with the unwell voice and what is driving it to motivate our choices, the easier it will be to allow our well voice to be the one to influence our decisions. Our first step is to build our relationship with our well voice.

At this early stage in your recovery, it's vital that you start to become conscious about the thoughts you are having and whether they are coming from a *well* or an *unwell* voice. For lots of people I work with, this is an alien concept to begin with – but once you consider the origin and intention of your thoughts, you'll begin to recognize that you have this push and shove going on in your head much of the time. At this point, you can begin to take back control by deciding not to listen to the unwell voice.

If you struggle to work out which voice is which, next time you have a thought, ask yourself: *Is this thought leading me to harm myself in some way?*

Your unwell voice is directing you to harm and punish yourself, emotionally and physically (and it is actively discouraging you from acting in your best interests).

Self-punishment, self-destruction and self-harm can each take many different forms. Here are a just a few examples:

- **Emotional harm**: Talking to yourself in a way that makes you feel sad, lonely and worthless.
- **Physical harm**: Restricting food, cutting yourself, over-exercising, denying yourself adequate sleep, or abusing alcohol or drugs.
- **Harmful actions**: Maintaining relationships with abusive people, acting out sexually, stealing, or lying to people.

One important thing to note: don't try to negotiate with your unwell voice. As a young person I was locked in this battle for years, so I know how tempting it is, but arguing with your unwell voice merely gives it value and power. For example, the voice would tell me that I shouldn't see friends because I was anxious and I would make them feel uncomfortable. I would internally respond by saying that my friends loved me and understood I was having a hard time. But any self-compassion or hint of a challenge angered the unwell voice, and prompted even more vicious attacks. I also discovered that when you ignore the unwell voice, it shouts louder – and so I realized that a more neutral response was the key.

Instead of negotiating or ignoring the unwell voice, simply try to acknowledge its words without engaging with it, bartering with it or acting on its demands. I know this is a big ask, particularly if you're very used to doing whatever that unwell voice says, and especially as changing habits and thought patterns rarely come easily, but with practice you can do this.

Learning to tolerate the unwell voice without reacting to it is one of the biggest first steps you can take, and this will serve not only to weaken this voice's power but also to help you kick-start the recovery process and begin to reclaim your life. This process of recovery and healing will enable you to:

- Navigate the world with calm and clarity of thought.
- Form intimate and nurturing relationships with yourself and others.
- Understand that your thoughts are just your perspective, and not necessarily reality.
- Connect with your creative self and allow yourself to play.
- Forgive yourself and others.
- Accept criticism without internalizing the views of others as your own 'truth'.
- Become empowered and masterful within your own life.

Recovery is not linear; it's a challenging process that involves being faced with various challenging situations and experiences, which you can reflect upon as opportunities to continue to grow and progress. A good day can often be followed by a more difficult day. Healing is about working through the layers that are uncovered as you make your way through this process.

It's important at this point to be mindful that it's still early days and healing takes time, so try not to be tempted to be overly critical of your progress. The shifts that you will experience are something that you are only likely to be able to reflect on and feel at a deeper level over a period of time. So while the changes might be small at first, these stack up and give way to much greater shifts.

Try to focus on what you are investing in your recovery, as opposed to what you are getting 'out' of it. With time you will see the benefits of your investment in yourself, and experience a more joyful and peaceful existence.

#HealHack

Take your time – this process is about putting one foot in front of the other. The changes that you are going to experience may seem like small shifts, but it's with rocks that we build mountains.

Step 2: Spot Your Coping Strategies

Choosing to place recovery and its positive,
affirming messages at the forefront of your
awareness has to be a very conscious choice.

In the early years of my recovery I found it very challenging to be able to identify areas in my life where I may have been stuck or acting out in a destructive way. It was only later, after years of studying psychotherapy and lots of introspection, that I came to recognize that some of my unwell behaviours had really been ways of trying to cope with and manage life. As we move forward together, I think it's worth spending some time getting curious about what your coping strategies might be and whether they're actually helping you ... I know for certain that mine weren't, and only by realizing that was I better able to resource myself for the future.

What is a coping strategy?

We've learned about our unwell voice and how it becomes established as a way of coping with the world we were raised in. But now let's delve into some of the specific strategies that we may be using to cope with challenging experiences and emotions. Do you know what yours are?

I'm talking here about those thoughts or behaviours that help you to manage the challenges of day-to-day life. When we begin to reflect on how we get through difficult life events, we may come to find that we've developed various strategies that appear to help us to cope but which actually contribute to keeping us trapped in a destructive and painful cycle.

We're now going to explore in further detail which coping strategies might be negative, and how we can identify and develop more nurturing tools for coping.

What are destructive coping strategies?

Self-destructive behaviour comes in many guises – some extreme, some not so extreme. An extreme form of self-destructive behaviour might be sabotaging yourself by not going into work, knowing you will get fired if you don't. A less extreme example might be picking a fight with a friend.

Maladaptive coping skills are ways of dealing with stress that can often exacerbate feelings of low self-worth – and, in many cases, make a situation worse. These types of coping strategies can hurt your social relationships, make pre-existing problems worse, and even result in new distresses.

Some examples of destructive coping strategies are:

- **Critical self-talk**: Saying to yourself, *I'm stupid, ugly, worthless,* etc.
- **Restrictive eating**: Constant dieting or starving yourself.
- **Bingeing/overeating**: Bingeing on foods you've labelled as 'bad'.
- **Neglecting self-care activities**: Never making time to do the things that make you feel good.
- **Pursuing abusive relationships with others**: Repeatedly going back to the same people, hoping that they will show you the love or affection that you crave, and experiencing the same rejection time after time.

- **Drug and alcohol abuse**: Turning to drugs and alcohol as a way of avoiding and numbing feelings.
- **Compulsive gaming**: A tool to disconnect from reality, because life is too painful.
- **Self-injury**: Harming yourself physically as a way of trying to relieve emotional pain.
- **Self-pity**: Getting entrenched in a 'victim' mentality, which leaves you feeling impotent and powerless.
- **Rejecting help**: Indulging in destructive strategies because you are scared of 'doing the work' required to change.
- **Overspending**: Creating scenarios to facilitate further anxiety, because you are unconsciously motivated to stay feeling bad.
- **Sabotaging relationships**: Avoiding intimacy and vulnerability at all costs.
- **Gossiping about others**: Seeking flaws in others to feel better about your low self-worth.
- **Social isolation**: Avoiding connection with others because you cannot bear to be seen.

It's important to recognize that all disordered behaviours are destructive and that self-healing involves leaving *all* of the symptoms behind, not just the one we think we engage in the most. In order to do that, we have to put our recovery first and make it part of how we live. After all, that's what low self-worth does – it impacts every aspect of

our lives – so let's be just as thorough and tenacious about recovery.

Many of us get drawn into trying not to act out on behaviours we have identified as negative – for example, trying not to overeat 'bad' foods. But my experience with this was that every time I tried not to do something destructive, I felt as though I was white-knuckling it and that I was a pressure cooker that was going to explode – and so often, the fallout was epic.

A better strategy is to combine minimizing those harmful behaviours with investing in expanding positive tools for coping, so that the destructive strategies become redundant. Of course, if we don't witness self-care and self-compassion being modelled by our parent figures in childhood, these things can feel very difficult to implement in adulthood. But the recovery tools I've developed in this book are a clear way of helping you to do this.

Managing your healing on a daily basis

Put your recovery first

I find that when many people begin the process of self-healing, they initially don't invest enough in change and then are disappointed when things don't change. Recovery and self-healing are about more than just attending a one-hour therapy session, or reading a book like this. It's about completely transforming how you treat yourself and how you live your life.

When I first tell people how important it is to integrate recovery – and all those healthier messages and ways of being – into their daily lives, I'm often met with the complaint 'I don't want to think about it all the time!' I understand this, of course – the urge to disconnect from ourselves can be enticing – but as so many of us are living with our unwell voice all the time, it must be tackled all the time.

Look at it this way: your unwell voice is giving you a hard time every single day, from the minute you wake up until the minute you go to bed. Imagine what life could be like if you started replacing that negative perception of yourself and your life with a sense of hope, joy and recovery – a belief that you can take care of and nurture yourself, instead of hurting and punishing yourself.

Choosing to place recovery and its positive, affirming messages at the forefront of your awareness has to be a very conscious choice. As a result, it may feel arduous and unfamiliar at first, and maybe even 'wrong'. But that's just because you've become so used to living with your unwell thoughts that they've become entirely natural and embedded in your unconscious. Soon, though, if you practise it enough, hearing your well voice and putting your recovery and wellbeing first (rather than succumbing to your unwell voice's demands) will become a vital part of how you live your life.

Finding healthier ways of coping

We will be working towards a place where you are able to develop multiple new tools to nurture your body and your mind. In the process of doing this, it can be helpful to think of your destructive coping strategies and the unwell thoughts and behaviours as an 'acting out' of your feelings.

What this means is that, instead of observing the feelings, sitting with them or watching them emerge and recede, we enact them with a behaviour. This can be a hard concept to grasp, especially when certain behaviours have become knee-jerk reactions.

Let's look at the example of one of my clients, Sarah, who had feelings of low self-worth and lacked confidence in most areas of her life. She suffered with social anxiety, and self-isolation and avoidance had become strategies she used to try to manage that anxiety. Over the years she had become so focused on trying to manage her anxiety that she'd never stopped to reflect on and consider the origins of her feelings of low self-worth.

When Sarah started recovery, she was guided to consider *why* she felt so negative about herself, and she came to uncover that many of these feelings were rooted in childhood. She learned that her anxiety was really an expression of how she felt – and in developing other ways of expressing that feeling, Sarah was able to heal and to leave behind some of her 'old' coping tools.

Sarah's story is a good example of how turning to self-isolation and avoidance can provide a temporary sense of relief from symptoms of anxiety. But, ultimately, Sarah was left with feelings of sadness and self-loathing, and the root cause of those things wasn't being addressed.

Self-destructive behaviours are more likely to be implemented when you have a very negative view of yourself; the unwell voice thrives on low self-esteem. It is also fuelled by a person's sense of shame – there's a strong fear of being judged negatively by others, which makes it hard to reach out and seek help. Nobody in my clinic gets judged for having a damaged relationship with themselves; rather, they are taught how to develop a nurturing relationship, to respect and heal their body, and to live their life guided by compassion and kindness.

So, when you want to run and hide from that unwell voice or the pain you feel stirring within your heart . . . don't.

Sit. Breathe. Be.

Step 3: Work on Your Relationships

You can have intimacy or you can have control,
but you can't have both.

When people ask me what the commonalities are among the people that I work with, I always respond with the same thing: 'People who struggle to build or maintain intimate relationships with themselves and others.' So many of us are struggling to connect on a really deep and meaningful level with others, but we get so drawn into focusing on the wrong things that I think we often miss the bigger picture. People will tell me that they date the wrong people, that they can't meet anyone or that they remain trapped in unfulfilling relationships . . . but what they so often *don't* do is ask why. Why has having relationships become so challenging? Let's explore this together . . .

Trauma and relationships

When we are living with unprocessed trauma and we have developed a set of destructive coping strategies to try to manage, and to survive, our relationships are inevitably impacted, but it's vital to consider *why* we pursue relationships (both romantic connections and friendships) with certain people and how this came to be.

How we perceive relationships is first established in childhood, and we use the relationships that we have with our parents as the blueprint for how we expect things to be. The connection and bond that we experience as a baby go on to determine how we relate to other people throughout life and into adulthood. This blueprint establishes the foundation for all verbal and non-verbal communication in future relationships, and teaches us how the world will be.

When we experience trauma in childhood, we look to our primary caregivers to validate these experiences and guide us in how to cope with such events. If they either don't validate them or are not able to show us how to process them in a healthy way, we internalize our emotional responses and become stuck.

When we are living with unprocessed trauma, we unconsciously seek out opportunities to relive our childhood experiences with disengaged or potentially abusive partners who will then replicate those events. We are still looking for that validation and comfort from our parental figures, and often we find ourselves repeating patterns with partners who are unavailable, unable to form intimate relationships or are abusive to us.

So many of us are completely unaware that we are the ones driving these encounters. What we feel is a compulsion to pursue unhealthy relationships, even when we intuitively *know* that something isn't right, because we misconstrue familiarity as desire and chemistry. For example, someone asks you out on a date and there are lots of red flags you *could* acknowledge but you don't, so you ignore that the person is in another relationship/has alcohol issues/ignores your calls/has a history of abusive behaviour (take your pick) because something else is driving you to say yes.

What we're really doing here is acting out a need to revisit familiar wounds, in a quest to repair parental relationships. When this repairing doesn't happen, we tell ourselves that the problem is us: that we are flawed, inadequate and unworthy of love.

Conversely, in cases where there is an opportunity to explore a relationship with a more 'well' partner, we are often dismissive and disinterested. How many times have you heard (or said) the phrase 'I like them, I just don't fancy them'? Could this be translated to: 'That person is unlikely to abuse me in the way that I need to be abused in order to feel that any expression of love is real.'

Something powerful and unconscious is at work in our relationships, and in order for things to change we need to become more conscious and aware. In my clinic, almost without exception, my clients raise the following issues with regard to relationships:

- Unable to find a long-term intimate relationship
- Pattern of abusive relationships
- Absence of any physical relationships
- Bullying among friendship groups
- An inability to establish healthy boundaries in relationships. (What constitutes a 'healthy

boundary' can be a totally new concept for many of us, so we'll get into this in more depth in a short while.)
- Sabotaging of relationships
- An inability to nurture or sustain intimate relationships with others

If you are able to identify similar patterns in your own relationship history, then it's worth reflecting on this: *You* are the common denominator.

Now, this statement is not about blame. It's about giving you the opportunity to reflect on the possibility that you are playing an active part in seeking out these scenarios *because* of old, unresolved trauma.

Once we are able to take responsibility for the role that we are playing in the relationships that we have, we have an opportunity to galvanize change – because we come to realize that it is *us* who is capable of creating a shift in our lives.

Trauma and attachment styles

Attachment theory was developed by psychologist John Bowlby in the 1950s and '60s, and in essence describes different ways in which one is able to relate to others. Let's take a moment to explore these:

Insecure-avoidant or dismissive-avoidant attachment style

If you are raised in an environment where your parents or caregivers ignore or are unresponsive to your wants and needs, you may form an insecure-avoidant or dismissive-avoidant attachment style. This means that you are going to find it very challenging to form any close relationships with people, and will likely avoid any sort of intimacy. You are likely to be secretive, shutting down when others open up or show emotion. Underneath these defences, you are desperate for connection and struggle with feeling alone.

Fearful-avoidant or disorganized-disoriented attachment style

Those who have experienced persistent physical and/or emotional abuse are likely to develop this attachment style. When the person that you are raised by – who is supposed to love and care for you – is the person that hurts you, you grow up to fear both intimacy and being alone. You will find it hard to trust people, will detach yourself from others emotionally, and will be terrified of being vulnerable or showing affection.

Insecure-ambivalent or anxious-preoccupied attachment style

This attachment style emerges when parents or caregivers are inconsistent with how they respond to your needs. They fluctuate between being responsive and ignoring or neglecting them. Under these circumstances, you will grow up feeling 'clingy' and anxious in relationships with others. You are likely to crave intimacy but then develop hypervigilant traits with regards to 'monitoring' the behaviour of your partner. You are likely to feel jealous, insecure and paranoid.

It can be useful to consider whether you are able to identify with any of these attachment styles, because just by becoming mindful of how our trauma may have impacted our ability to form relationships, we are then able to challenge some of these toxic patterns.

A point I think it's vital to flag here is that it can be very difficult to look back at our own childhood objectively and be able to make these assessments of our own attachment style. So much of this material can be subtle and hard to identify. I have had several painful blows dealt to me over the years in the form of 'reality checks' delivered by therapists. I refer to this process as 'waking up', because it's only when we do that that we can really 'see' what we've been through and recognize own our experiences and our truth.

Healing your heart

What we are aiming to achieve is to establish a 'secure' attachment style. This is where you are able to:

- Communicate openly and constructively.
- Respond to others with empathy.
- Establish and maintain healthy boundaries.
- Express and receive physical intimacy appropriately.
- Feel secure within yourself.
- Negotiate conflict through compromise.

Having a secure attachment style does not mean that you never experience challenges in relationships, but it does mean that you are able to process difficult events, grieve as necessary and move on successfully.

Giving yourself the opportunity to explore and gain a deeper insight into early childhood experiences that may have influenced your attachment style can help you to improve your relationships as an adult.

When I begin this work with my clients, and we start to explore attachment styles and the obstacles that have prevented them from embracing intimate relationships, the biggest challenge is overcoming the intense fear they have of change. As damaging as these early behaviours may have been, they are at least familiar – and there is something comfortable about staying put! Now is your time to be brave and begin to tentatively venture into uncharted waters. Just remember it will be okay, and that we can take those first steps slowly and together.

Many people's instinct when they realize that historically they've been drawn to the wrong partners is to set up an internal 'high alert' station, where they view any prospective new friendships or partners with acute suspicion and wariness. There is a fear that if they allow themselves to be vulnerable it will 'all just happen again'.

But it's not going to play out like that. Exploring new relationships is not about being entirely vulnerable, and nor is it about being entirely defended. Oversharing prematurely or surrounding ourselves with a metaphorical fort will just serve to alienate us from people and reinforce a sense of separation or loneliness.

By trying to 'protect' ourselves, we are actually blocking any chance of building healthy relationships with anyone.

What we can learn to do is to establish boundaries (see Recovery Tool: Setting and Maintaining Boundaries on pp. 195–200), which will communicate to people what we will or won't tolerate. Boundaries also create a safety net so we can venture out and let people in, but at a pace that feels measured and safe.

One of the best ways of knowing that you are attracting the 'right' kind of romantic partner is to consider the relationship that you have with yourself. When you know that you are treating yourself with love, respect and kindness, then you can trust that you are communicating to the rest of the world that this is what you expect and deserve from others.

#HealHack

Take a moment to reflect and identify times when you know you acted against your own instincts or intuition. When we look back, so often we become aware that there was a present voice or feeling that tried to guide us, but we ignored it. By doing this exercise it will help to give you the confidence that, deep inside you somewhere, you *know* how to take care of yourself.

Recovery Tool: Cultivate an Attitude of Gratitude

When I look back on the pain that I've experienced in my life, this may sound really strange but I now see it as a gift. It was excruciating to experience it and I would never want to return to it, but in retrospect I can see that I've gained so much from it. When things are challenging, so many of us can become bogged down in a negative cycle where we feel like a passenger in our own life, but this book is about you becoming an empowered creator of your own reality – and the truth is that the more gratitude you are able to cultivate towards your own life, the more you will attract what you want, whether that's a romantic relationship, a more fulfilling career or prosperous lifestyle.

If we start the day with resentment, worry and fear, we'll quickly find that those feelings snowball and generate more of the same. Gratitude is a Patronus against self-pity and disempowerment; it increases feelings of positivity, and prompts us to form habits of expressing thankfulness and appreciation in all parts of our lives. Gratitude enables us to let go of the focus on and aversion to what we have but don't want, and to start to 'feel' better.

Daily gratitude lists

Begin the day by writing a list of three things that you are grateful for, proud of or excited about in your life. In painful times, you might have to work hard to unearth the positive, but if you look, you will find it.

Here are some basic examples that might help get your gratitude vibes going:

- Clean water to drink
- A friend to talk to
- Your home or a place you feel safe
- Books, for adding wisdom into your life
- The sun for providing life and warmth
- Your legs for allowing you to walk, run, dance and play
- Your eyes, to read this book

If you find you are stuck in a negative place or a difficult situation, then you can always shift your perspective to see it more positively. Let's look at a few examples:

- *You've lost your job*: You feel grateful for the opportunity to start over, and think about what you might like to do next.
- *You've ended a relationship*: You feel grateful for the freedom of being single, and the excitement of meeting new people.

- *Feeling physically unwell*: You're grateful for the parts of your body that are working well.
- *Someone behaves badly towards you*: You're grateful to be reminded of how important it is to be loving towards others.

When faced with adversity, it's a challenge for any of us to recognize these 'gifts' as they are playing out, but retrospectively we are able to see that there is always something to learn – and, thus, something for which we can be grateful.

Share the love

Through cultivating an attitude of gratitude, you will be able to develop a fundamental belief that the world is good and is there to serve you. Acknowledging and welcoming all of life's experiences will help you to find flow within your daily life, and you will be able to translate this joy into discovery and soul growth.

Don't be afraid to share your sense of gratitude with others. Acknowledge when other people have touched your life, and thank them for inspiring, loving, listening or supporting you. So often we reflect on what we wish we had said to people once they are no longer with us and it is too late. Make the simple and conscious choice to open your heart and tell those around you why you appreciate them.

Step 4: Empowering the Self

Recovery is about connecting with
who you really are and all you feel passionate about.

The journey of healing is all about focusing on what we want – and what we need to change in order to achieve it. Often we don't fight for the life we really want because we have told ourselves it's not possible, and we allow these limiting thoughts to keep us stifled. By illuminating our own truths, we are able to embrace life with an invigorated enthusiasm because we know what we want, what we're capable of and who we really are.

We need to look at this work really holistically. This isn't just about feeling better . . . it's an opportunity to embrace something truly transformational and inspirational. To become truly alive and awakened in every sense.

It's time to get curious about where we're being held back.

What areas of your life is your unwell voice impacting?

Recovery isn't just about acknowledging and under-standing how an unwell voice literally sounds and manifests — it's also about noticing all those areas of your life that it is compromising or damaging.

Even if you think it's not all that bad, I promise you that your unwell voice is holding you back from being the very best version of yourself. It is a destructive force that inevit-ably impacts romantic partnerships and relationships with family and friends, as well as academic choices and career moves. It isolates and punishes you, preventing you from following your dreams and having aspirations by keeping you trapped in a place of fear.

As well as providing a constant stream of self-critical thoughts, the unwell voice can also lead you to behave in ways that increase your sense of shame and resentment towards others. For example, it can cause you to:

- Dislike seeing others succeed.
- Compare yourself to others.
- Feel threatened by other people's success.
- Gossip about others.
- Be critical of the way others look.
- Feel superior to/better than others.

All of these behaviours are tools that the unwell voice uses to deepen a sense of self-loathing and shame. But they can also be healed.

Your recovery is not only going to involve leaving these thoughts and behaviours behind, but also embracing a more nurturing and loving relationship with yourself on every level. Recovery is a process of personal empowerment – so it's time to get curious about all the areas of your life where there's space for you to heal, and where you might better nurture yourself. This means exploring how you communicate with your friends and family, and beginning to consider how (and how much) you typically express and articulate your needs.

For so many of us, life has become little more than a question of survival – of getting from one day to the next. So often when I ask people how they are doing, their response will be 'not bad' . . . as if that's a good thing! Why have we come to have such low expectations of life and what we can hope to get out of it?

When you're in the clutches of an unwell voice, there's no scope for thinking creatively about who you want to be or what you want in your future. Why? Because your daily existence is consumed by thoughts of self-doubt and self-ridicule, as well as controlling behaviours that limit your ability to thrive.

In this chapter we are going to look at whether your career, studies or self-development pursuits are connecting you with parts of yourself that exude passion and creativity. This also means considering what you really care about, and what you really love.

For long enough now, your unwell voice has operated like a dense fog that's eclipsed your essence. Recovery is about connecting with who you really are and all you feel passionate about. Living with this voice is like living with the very worst kind of bully – one that undermines you constantly, telling you that you're not capable, your loneliness is inevitable and you're not good enough. It will have deliberately facilitated situations where your worst fears are realized, and it will have continued to condition you by feeding you negative thought after negative thought until self-confidence and self-belief seem like totally impossible concepts.

This is all going to change. Throughout your recovery you will gain confidence, courage and a self-belief that will empower and energize you. I know it might seem too good to be true, but I promise you that *transformation really is possible*.

Yes, at this stage, the very thought of changing might be scary, even if you know that's what you want. Destructive patterns can appear to hold us in place and represent a (misplaced) kind of safety. But look at it this way, perhaps: you've invested so much trust in a voice that has only been there to hurt you. It has *not* kept you safe, and it has suffocated your emotional and spiritual growth. Its primary interest has been about keeping you trapped in this hellish place; it's caused you untold amounts of pain and sadness, and it's time for that to stop.

Getting inspired

Until now, everything you've thought yourself capable of has been viewed through the lens of what you *believe* you are capable of – a filter of poor self-confidence and low self-esteem. Let's start thinking about what possibilities might exist for you if you didn't have this pervasive self-doubt.

If you didn't feel so bad about yourself, what would you do? Where would you go? What would you love to pursue? I know this can be difficult to think about – for many of us, our unwell voice becomes entrenched in our most formative years, and therefore we've never had much space to consider these things at all. But trust me: you can achieve things for yourself that are far more wonderful than anything you've thought possible in the past. Give yourself permission simply to allow yourself to dream, and see what comes up! The biggest hurdle for you to overcome on this journey is your lack of self-belief, but you *can* and *will* heal.

Fear-based thinking

Over the many years that I've done this kind of work, I've found some common things crop up. One that happens time and again is people saying it feels foolish to imagine the life of their dreams – that they'd be kidding themselves if they thought it might be possible, and then they'd just get disappointed by reality.

I call this 'fear-based thinking'. It's exactly the kind of thinking that stops any of us fighting for the change we want to create. So many of us look back at past experiences in order to get a sense of what we feel we can achieve in the future, but if you've been living with an unwell voice that's consumed so much of you every day (putting you down, telling you you're nothing, and so on), how can your past possibly be a measure of what you're capable of?

What's more – if you *have* achieved things you're proud of, *in spite of* living with that unwell voice, just think how much *more* you will be capable of when you become a well and happy person who can identify what you want and go out and get it!

It can feel disheartening when we look back and realize that we've been living with an unwell voice for a long time. Lots of people feel an understandable sadness when they think how much time they've wasted while being dictated to by this voice, but I'd encourage you to look back on your journey so far as a vital learning experience from which you will draw much wisdom.

You are strong and resilient, and these gifts will serve you now and for the rest of your life (I promise). Even if you aren't there yet, you will one day feel gratitude for the opportunities offered to you by the years consumed by this self-doubt – namely, the chance to enter the process of recovery, which is all about aiming for things you want, fighting for better relationships with yourself and others and nurturing yourself.

Now is the time to find the strength within you to pursue things that you really want to do! Both the childish and the aspirational parts of yourself – which have probably never (or not recently, anyway) been given permission to do what they really want – are going to get a chance not only to express themselves, but also to make those dreams a reality.

Witnessing your fear

If the idea of changing and working on every part of your life feels daunting, that's unsurprising. Fear plagues many of us, and for those of us living with an unwell voice it's pretty much ever-present. Fear might present itself as a low-level constant hum, or it might show up only when triggered by a thought (perhaps one that then leads us down a path of negative self-belief or self-destruction, or causes a panic attack in the moment).

Our relationship with fear is all dependent on how much faith we place in fear itself. It's important here to consider the actual purpose of fear in our lives. What is fear there for? Really, it's about keeping us safe. For example, being fearful about stepping out into oncoming traffic or putting our hand in a flame is useful fear that will stop us from getting hurt. But so many of us seem to have become stuck with a fear-based mentality that goes way beyond being useful.

At some point, we adopted the belief that we must always be very cautious; we must live in this fearful way because if we don't, then something bad will happen. This might be a way of thinking that we've inherited or been actively taught by our parental figures, or it could be one we've absorbed while growing up. I was always fearful of trying new things because I was so avoidant of failure, but I've come to realize that there is value in the experience – regardless of the outcome.

Excessive fear is unnecessary and debilitating. It holds

us back from fulfilling our potential, and ultimately limits our happiness, *a lot*. When we map out our lives from the position of a fear-based belief system, we end up re-creating scenarios from a place of what feels familiar, a somewhat self-fulfilling prophecy. Our fears might not only play out in front of our eyes, but we might also project those fears onto the future.

Detaching from fear

One of the first steps in detaching from fear-based thinking is to identify these thoughts as another facet of our unwell voice. Just as we're learning to recognize the difference between well and unwell thoughts, so we can begin to associate these fear-driven thoughts with that unwell voice.

One thing I often hear people say when I suggest they start to detach from fear-based thoughts is: 'But bad things do happen, so the fear is necessary!' What I tell them in return is that letting go of fear isn't about securing a future where nothing 'bad' or challenging ever happens – it's about trusting that we're on a path where what is right for us won't pass us by.

Of course, life can still be difficult or painful. But when it is, I continue to trust that there's a lesson in the experience – something I can learn from. When things I thought I wanted don't work out the way I hoped, I trust that they were never meant for me. Amazingly (or perhaps inevitably), there's often something more worthwhile waiting around the corner.

Fear-based thinking doesn't prevent loss and pain. What's more, it never will. The reality is that loss does impact our lives in all sorts of ways, most of which we can't control and some of which we don't yet know. That's quite hard to accept sometimes and can leave us with a fair bit of uncertainty, but one thing I know from my own experience is if I choose to live life with an open heart – and I trust that the universe will deliver what's meant for me – I'll get the things I need. If that feels a little 'woo-woo' to you, don't worry, I felt that way too a long time ago. Stick with it, and give this new way of thinking a chance.

Recognizing patterns of fear

Patterns of fear will dictate our behaviours and control our emotions – until they are identified and challenged. When you become an honest witness to your fear, you can begin to notice how it shows up in your life. You'll find that it will typically arrive in certain situations and at predictable times. Many of your fear patterns have probably been established for such a long time that they run in the background, without you even being particularly aware of them. As you become conscious of them, and begin to identify your patterns, you can get closer to the precise moment where your fear takes hold, and then you can choose to stand your ground in the face of that fear and react another way.

For example, if you recognize that your fear shows up any time you're asked to go somewhere new (and you tell yourself things like *I'm too busy to go out, I'm going to feel stupid if I go* or *I have nothing to wear*), you'll start to see how your fear operates. It may look like it's protecting you, but in reality it's not. This kind of fear is just about low self-esteem – it's about you not feeling good enough – and the more we feed the fear, the bigger it usually gets.

Responding to these fear-based thoughts with a positive affirmative mantra can really help. For example:

Unwell Voice: 'I have nothing to wear.'
Affirmative Voice: 'I am worthy and good enough.'

Awareness is the precursor to change, because with awareness comes choice. The better we get to know our patterns and responses to triggers, the more we'll be able to recognize which thoughts are truly of service to us and which are holding us back.

I see fear as another form of the unwell voice, and a barrier to recovery. When we are witnessing our patterns, we are stepping back and disengaging a little from what has triggered our fear. As we detach from fear, we create space to connect with our higher selves, and the parts of us that are full of love and compassion. As the noise of fear subsides, we're able to tune in to a different internal voice: our well and wise voice. We may have been unaware of this voice throughout our lives up until this point, but now it can be heard.

Techniques to tackle fear

Speak your fear out loud

When you feel your thinking becoming clouded by fear, try speaking your particular fear out loud. Sometimes it's a question of calling a friend and sharing whatever it is you're frightened of. This works because fear tends to hold a lot more weight when it's protected by silence.

Voicing fears out loud (ideally to someone else, but you can also say them to yourself in the mirror) often has the strange effect of lessening their impact so that you're able to see them for what they really are – just facets of that unwell voice, and only worth observing rather than reacting to.

Remember you are not your thoughts

We are not what we *think* we are; we are not our thoughts. Everything that we see in the world and in ourselves is through the filter of our own perception.

With this higher level of awareness, you can step outside yourself and watch how your mind drifts from one thought to another. You can begin to witness how you have formed habitual reactions to certain thoughts, but that you also have a choice. You can allow the thought to just 'be'; you don't *have* to react to it.

Stop comparing

Comparisons keep us trapped in a place of fear. We use comparisons as a way of either validating our unwell choices – *Well, others do it, so I'm fine* – or making ourselves feel bad: *She's younger than me and she's already married.*

The journey that I'm guiding you on throughout this book is about you celebrating who you are, and not looking outside yourself for validation. The unwell voice likes us to feel separate from others, and it weakens our connection to our own healing. Comparison really is an attack on ourselves, and it is unhelpful and unproductive, but it is also something that, with practice, we can consciously stop doing. Simply becoming conscious about our tendency to compare ourselves is often enough to change it.

Be mindful of judgement

So many people that I've worked with over the years have become drawn into a habit of using judgement as a tool for self-comfort. We judge others when we are feeling hurt and insecure, as a way of trying to make ourselves feel better. But the truth is, when we judge others we are engaging in toxic behaviour that actually drains our energy and empathy.

Fear harnesses judgement and uses it to separate us from others, which leaves us feeling empty and lonely. We all get drawn back into making judgements at times, but just be mindful of when this happens so you can bring yourself back to a more accepting place.

Get creative

When you feel that swell of fear rising, give yourself permission to take a break and engage in something creative. Fear ensures that we are continually standing still, by convincing us that it's a safe place to be. But we will never be satisfied living life in this way. There is so much of your creative self that has yet to unfold, and living in fear stifles this part of yourself and doesn't allow you to explore who you really are.

So start drawing, writing, painting, singing or expressing yourself creatively in whatever way feels organic to you. And if you're not sure what that is yet, allow yourself to experiment and see what works. If you find yourself feeling cautious, then ask yourself what you're afraid of . . . explore your fear: *If I wasn't afraid of being judged, what would I do?*

Fear shuts down our ability to live a full life. It stops us exploring the world and ourselves. Life can be beautiful

and rewarding – not because it's perfect and unflawed, but because there is love and reward in adversity and failure. There are opportunities for growth and development to be found in rejection and pain. There is beauty in loss and endings. Our strength comes from the rising above – from becoming empowered where we once felt fear.

Turn towards what scares you; it is there that you will find yourself.

#HealHack

Keep a blank notepad in your bag or somewhere near you during the day. Use this as a space to doodle or write down your thoughts, whenever the mood takes you.

Recovery Tool:
Create a Vision Board

What is a vision board?

Vision boards are wonderful ways to boost your motivation for recovery and enhance your mood and focus. A vision board is a collection of words and images that inspire and motivate you, and generally make you feel good. Creating a vision board gives you an opportunity to explore, visualize and depict your goals and dreams in all of the core areas of your life. You can use very literal images, such as images of a particular house or space you want to live in, or take a more conceptual or abstract approach (for example, colours that inspire a certain mood or feeling). The key thing is to make sure that, when you look at your completed vision board, you feel excited and hopeful about what the future holds.

A vision board is a great tool for helping you manifest all of the changes that you want to make in your life, because when we are able to visualize something that we want, we are far more likely to achieve it.

Once you've created your board, put it up somewhere prominent that allows you to see it every day.

How to design your board

Often, when my clients begin designing their boards, they go a bit blank. It's hard sometimes to envisage your dreams when you've been stuck in self-hatred or negative thinking.

I've put together the following tips to help get you started:

1. Consider dividing your board into five sections: relationships, career/education, home, travel and inspiration.

2. For the **relationships** section, think about these questions: Who would you like to meet or spend your time with? What kind of relationships would you like to have with yourself and other people? What do you want from a partner? Do you want children? Or pets?

3. For the **career/education** section, consider including images to do with career paths, vocations or courses that you might be interested in or which you might aspire to. Don't worry if you're not certain about what you want to do in the future or what you'd like to learn; this is meant to be a fun experience where you get to play with ideas. (If you put something on your board now that doesn't feel right later, you can just take it off.)

4. For the **home** section, it's often fun to find images of any kinds of homes that you can see yourself living in! Again, this isn't about deciding exactly what you want, but rather giving yourself permission to explore your future. (At one time I had a town house, a loft apartment *and* a country cottage on my board.) Sometimes when we allow ourselves the freedom to entertain all possibilities, what we really want becomes clearer.

5. For the **travel** section, collect images of places that you'd love to visit one day.

6. Your **inspiration** section is a free space for anything that makes you feel inspired or

motivated. I always include images of women who I see doing great things, and quotes that encourage me to be the best version of myself.

#HealHack

Remember to write the date on the back of your vision board once you've made it. It's great to hold on to old vision boards and look at them later, once you've started to do the things you dreamed of; there's a real satisfaction in seeing what you've accomplished – and knowing that you can achieve anything you believe is within reach.

Step 5: Identify Your Trauma

*Shame is an emotion that arises when
we judge ourselves at our core in a negative light.*

**Take a deep breath. You've made it this far, and at
this point it's my job to tell you that you are a courageous human being (despite what that unwell voice
might have said). You are challenging yourself to do
some incredibly restorative and loving work on yourself, and that is a real act of bravery.**

**We're now going to take some time to look at
identifying trauma and the shame that keeps so
many of us trapped. This is an opportunity to gain
further wisdom and insight into your own journey –
remember to be kind to yourself, and take things at
your own pace.**

*Acknowledging internal shame and
healing internal wounds*

As we've already established, so many people are unaware
that they are living with an unwell voice that needs to be
challenged. They often don't seek help until they reach a
crisis point – when their anxiety becomes unmanageable

or their depression becomes debilitating. That leaves most people just coping and never really doing very much to address the impact that the unwell voice is having upon their lives.

Even when they do engage with professional support, many counselling and therapeutic treatment programmes focus on minimizing what are regarded as the main symptoms of the 'presenting problem' – in other words, helping a client to 'manage' their anxiety or depressive symptoms. For lots of people, this can be a terrifying process. And what these treatment strategies aren't necessarily considering is that many of these 'symptoms' have long been established as a way of coping with emotions; when these mechanisms are suddenly removed or threatened, people are left feeling extremely vulnerable and exposed.

I'd like to introduce you now to a past client of mine called Isla. A thirty-one-year-old woman, Isla was working in PR and liked her job, although it was often stressful and she worked long hours. Isla had been struggling with anxiety for several years, but recently her symptoms had escalated and she'd been signed off sick from work. Her GP had prescribed antidepressants and she'd attended a course of cognitive behavioural therapy (CBT) sessions at her local surgery. But Isla was feeling worse than ever and had come to me in desperation for help.

In our time together I discovered that Isla's self-esteem was at rock bottom; she felt like a total failure for having to take time off work and couldn't see a way forward. When we began to talk about Isla's anxiety, what was unearthed was actually a very strong and dictatorial unwell voice.

The themes of Isla's unwell voice centred heavily around her work, and sounded like this:

'You need to work as hard as you possibly can to succeed.'
'If you don't prove yourself at work, you'll be fired.'
'People think you're lazy and stupid.'

These unwell thoughts left Isla feeling incredibly ashamed, 'less than', anxious and very stressed. She tried to 'manage' the anxiety the unwell voice created by working late – becoming exhausted and putting an enormous amount of pressure on herself in the process. When we began to separate Isla from her unwell thoughts, she was able to recognize that they were a negative internal narrative that had become entrenched. With this insight, and an increasing confidence in investing in a more compassionate well voice, Isla began to gain strength and saw her anxiety symptoms diminish.

People who are living with an unwell voice are often plagued by a constant sense of internal and external shame. Internal shame is how a sufferer feels inside. Often it includes seeing themselves as flawed, inferior, pointless and unattractive. There might be a prevalent sense of feeling 'bad', as though they have done something very wrong.

External shame, on the other hand, is what's projected outwards. This is what the sufferer feels about others, and their fears about the outside world – for example, someone may be anxious about how they are perceived, perhaps believing that others see them as flawed, inferior, point-less and unattractive.

Time and again in my work I've come across clients who fear being exposed or 'found out' for who they really are and thus rejected from society. This external shame fuels the sufferer's desire to isolate themselves and hide from the world.

When one client bravely shared their experience of shame with me, they said:

> *I have spent a lifetime despising myself for all of my coping mech-anisms, dysfunctional behaviours and mental health struggles. I really believed that they were integral to who I am as a per-son. I felt so ashamed for being what I perceived as incapable and inadequate, and I really believed that I was both mad and bad. I not only minimized my childhood experiences, but largely blamed myself for them. I was so scared of having therapy because I couldn't bear the idea of another person being witness to my darkest truths and confirming my worst fears about myself, but coming to under-stand that the shame I've felt was a response to the traumas I've experienced has been so illuminating and healing.*

It's important at this point to draw a clear distinction between 'shame' and 'guilt', because the two are often so closely associated:

- **Shame** is an emotion that arises when we judge ourselves at our core in a negative light. For example, we may have had certain traumatic experiences that leave us with a deeply negative

sense of ourselves, or we may view ourselves as
'weak' or 'bad'.

- **Guilt** is an emotion that arises when we judge
our behaviour or actions in a negative way. For
example, if we are late for something and let
somebody down, then we may feel guilt for not
considering the impact our actions might have on
another person.

Shame and guilt influence our behaviour in different ways.
Guilt can motivate us to make amends, apologize or cor-
rect a behaviour. Doing such things will help alleviate our
guilt, and may increase the extent to which we feel positive
about ourselves. In this way, guilt can be a helpful emotion. Shame, however, is not productive. It silences and
isolates us, and that is why it is important to be able to dis-
tinguish between the two.

Sometimes we need to look backwards to move forwards. Rather than just focusing on restorative work in
therapy, where we aim to repair some of these damaging,
shame-based beliefs, it's important to also consider their
origins and thus what I call 'the core of the problem'.

Studies have consistently found a strong association
between shame and the destructive coping strategies we
engage in following a traumatic event. Because the experience of shame is often related to our own self-perceived
weakness or feelings of low worth, we are often too
ashamed about who we are and how we've behaved to
seek help and support.

I believe that unprocessed trauma lies at the core of who

we are for many people, and until they have learned constructive ways of coping with that trauma and processing the associated emotions, their symptoms will somehow still be serving a purpose – and so they will continue to struggle to relinquish their unwell voice and the associated destructive behaviours.

What is trauma?

When I initially ask my clients in the clinic about their trauma history, many deny having experienced trauma at all. This is hardly ever because they haven't experienced it, though, but rather because they aren't aware that their experiences would or could be regarded as traumatic.

When people think of trauma, they often conjure up images of people who've been through wars or other horrific events and who suffer from post-traumatic stress disorder. But when I talk about trauma, I'm not necessarily referring to PTSD (although with some people it is involved). 'Trauma' in my world refers to any traumatic event that has either happened to you directly or you have witnessed – anything that has overwhelmed you, that your system couldn't handle or process, and so has become an ongoing source of issues.

One example of a trauma that many people have experienced, but often don't think to mention at assessment stage, is the trauma of being bullied. Lots of people first experience bullying at school as children and then dismiss it. Yet these early experiences can have a profound impact on how we feel about ourselves, and the kind of relation-ships that we go on to form with others.

If we consider for a moment some of the common key shame-based beliefs, and then also look at the ways in which young people can be bullied, we can identify how those destructive core beliefs may have been established:

SHAME-BASED BELIEF	BULLYING LANGUAGE
I am flawed	'You're weird, there's something wrong with you'
I am inferior	'You're stupid'
I am pointless	'Why don't you kill yourself?'
I am unattractive	'You're fat and ugly'

As young people, we absorb the messages that we are given by those around us. Often these messages stay with us into adulthood, unchallenged. When those messages are from people whom we love and value, such as parents or primary caregivers, they become deeply entrenched in our psyches and actually dictate how we see ourselves as adults.

Some traumatic events and their impact will be easier to identify than others. For example, if someone has been in a car accident, they may be able to see clearly how that event impacted how they felt and the subsequent distress it caused. Other traumas are not so easy to discern. A more covert kind of trauma could be growing up in a household with parents who argue all the time. This can be very trau-matic for a child who doesn't understand the complexities of adult relationships and is unable to separate themselves from what is happening around them. Nevertheless, this particular trauma may not be something that immediately springs to mind when we start to reflect on the past.

When you feel safe enough, it's really important that you start to give some thought to the early wounds that you were exposed to. This may take a little time and consideration. When a trauma occurs in early childhood, many of us are unable to recall the details of the event – or may have no memories of it at all. As a result, we are unable to get a sense of who we were or what we were like before that trauma.

In other words, when your trauma occurs in childhood, you don't necessarily have a pre-trauma personality to compare your current behaviours against.

Contemplating your trauma is not only about spending time thinking or talking about painful memories; it is also about gaining context. One of the things that I see a lot in sufferers is the distress and confusion that arise when they simply cannot understand why they are in the position they're in.

People often say things like: 'I don't know why I'm like this – I had a great childhood.' Or: 'I don't have any trauma, so this must be all my fault.' Another common one is: 'There are people far worse off than me. I must be selfish for thinking my experiences were traumatic.'

Some of you may well recognize that you have been through damaging experiences, and you may be able to identify the impact that those events have had on your life, but I don't think I've ever met a client who doesn't feel on some level that either they deserved the traumas they've encountered or they were in some way responsible for what happened to them.

The majority of the people that I work with take full responsibility for their destructive actions, because they don't think there are any legitimate reasons to justify their unwell behaviours. But when you step back and take the time to look at the traumas in your journey, you can acknowledge the impact that these events had on the rest of your life.

Healing begins when we
honour and embrace our truth

This is not about comparing your experiences to anyone else's, but rather considering the impact they had on *you* and the messages that you have taken from those experiences.

In the clinic, when we first begin to look back at early trauma, many people will say, 'What's the point? We can't change the past!' Or they'll tell me, 'It's too painful, I can't do it.' And yes, it's true that we can't change the past, but that doesn't mean the past isn't worth investigating. We can learn valuable lessons from our early experiences, and even draw strength from them.

If you do decide to start considering early trauma, prioritizing your self-care is going to give you a solid foundation upon which you can do this. If you are able to work these things through with a therapist, then that's great, but connection to anyone during this time will help you. Trauma isolates us and disconnects us from our experiences, and connecting to yourself and others is going to play a big part in your healing.

This is very much a process to be worked on over a period of time, and in stages. Your primary focus needs to be on establishing a sense of safety. This is the cornerstone of your recovery; do not pressure yourself to talk about or disclose traumatic events.

I once worked with a client called Claire who found it challenging to connect or process past events, because she simply couldn't remember them. Here she describes her experience of connecting with herself:

When I began this journey of reflecting on some of my less-than-healthy coping tools and trying to develop a more compassionate self, I got really frustrated. I found it difficult to identify trauma in my own childhood and had very few memories of anything beyond a few birthday parties. I came to realize that because some of my early experiences were painful, my clever brain had decided not to form memories. I'd learned at a very young age to dissociate and disengage when things became uncomfortable. Healing does not require us to accurately remember everything. I just needed to accept that I had been impacted, and that was enough.

Just acknowledging your truth will go a long way to helping you feel safe and grounded.

The link between trauma and destructive coping strategies

The unwell voice can present various destructive coping strategies to deal with difficult and painful emotions. For those of you who are still struggling to identify or connect with a traumatic experience in your own lives, it's vital to understand that trauma can present in both overt and covert ways.

Young people who haven't experienced consistent love, care and nurturing can finish up with wounds as gaping as someone who has experienced a violent incident. It's important that you try not to compare your trauma to what others have been through, and instead acknowledge your individual journey and give it the attention that it needs and deserves.

Your unwell voice will likely rear its head around your trauma – and you will need to learn not to trust it when it does. It will likely tell you that what you have experienced is not a big deal, or that everyone has to deal with these things. And when it can't trivialize your experiences, it will blame you for them happening in the first place.

The more that we work at getting to know the difference between our well and unwell voices, the more likely it will be that we can predict how we will respond when we come to unpack these difficult memories and experiences – and then choose to respond with self-compassion.

For many of us, when we experience a trauma we unconsciously wish to be seen and heard, even if in the moment you might feel as though you want to hide away from the world. If you are anything like me, then you will have been desperate for comfort but also steeped in shame. The idea of anyone knowing what you've experienced or been through may be unimaginable at this stage. But rest assured this process needn't be about telling the world all about your life. It's more about your ability to acknowledge your experiences and trauma to yourself – that in itself can be massively healing, as can giving yourself permission to mourn and grieve so that you can move on.

I know it can seem terrifying, and that's why it's vital that you work at a pace that you feel comfortable with. There can be a temptation here to retreat back into those old coping strategies, but remember that your destructive coping tools do not actually keep you safe from the pain. After all, you've been living with it every day, haven't you? If anything, your destructive coping mechanisms have exacerbated that pain, by denying the severity of your early traumatic wounds and distracting you from your truth by getting you to focus your attention on external validation and landmark experiences, such as academic achievements and career promotions.

The relationship between our adult and child selves

Part of your recovery journey will be about acknowledging the wounded child within you (we'll go on to discuss the inner child later). Throughout our childhoods, if it has been difficult for us to take space, many of us will have stifled the positive childlike qualities and behaviours such as innocence, joy, sensitivity and creativity. Despite this, we hold within ourselves our inner child's hurts, fears and losses.

Our lack of connectedness to our inner child contributes to emotional difficulties in adult life because – although we have grown up – our wounded inner child has been unconsciously dictating many of our decisions, and those early wounds and traumas have remained unhealed.

Each of us has our own childhood experiences, and our inner child has stored the memory of those and their impact upon us. I believe that during our childhood years we form a kind of script, which informs all our future decisions and choices. The theory of life scripts is something that I've long been massively interested in, especially looking at my own life and the patterns I've been invested in. To me, life scripts are an undeniable truth, but they are also something we can change.

When I looked at my own life I saw repetitive patterns in friendships, romantic relationships and work, and the same dynamics were playing out time and time again . . . Only the players changed – well, except one. Me. And as I've said before, when you realize that you are the common denominator, it's time to accept that it is *you* that must change.

I came to understand that a life script is a subconscious life plan that we create in childhood through our interactions with our primary caregivers. We often have no idea that we've constructed this script or where it comes from, but it is powerful nonetheless and can impose destructive and unnecessary restrictions on our choices as adults.

So, the core messages that we absorb as children form the scripts that we unconsciously construct. These messages are from four different sources:

1. **Modelling:** In watching how others act and behave, we learn how we 'should' respond to the world. For example, we may learn from our parents that in our job we need to work long hours.

2. **Attributions:** Direct messages that we receive about who we are. For example, *you're lazy, lucky, careless, beautiful,* etc. We internalize these messages and they become part of how we see ourselves.

3. **Suggestions:** Statements that are made, often in the form of proclamations such as 'Practice makes perfect' or 'There's no such thing as failure'. We often find that we start to live by these rules.

4. **Injunctions:** These are more directive statements that we inherit from those around us. Examples are 'You'll never be rich' and 'There's no such thing as a happy marriage'.

There are of course positive examples of these messages that we absorb in childhood, but when they are negative they can seriously limit our life experiences and shape our future in a detrimental way. We can allow limiting beliefs and behaviours to define us, repeatedly making the same mistakes over and over again – which can leave us feeling powerless to change them.

It was only when I took a step back and observed the patterns in my own life – and learned about life scripts – that I realized history was repeating itself because my own life script was playing out over and over again.

When I'm first exploring life scripts with a client, I urge them to consider the patterns that they can identify in their own life and the messages that they perhaps absorbed as a child. We often have a sense of what we're afraid of, but we don't always know the origins of that fear.

'People always abandon me'

This is the fear that we will always be left by those we love and that we are powerless to stop it. We often have this fear before we are even engaged in a relationship; and, because of this established belief, we will often seek out people and scenarios that are more likely to fulfil this fear so that it becomes a self-fulfilling prophecy.

For example, we might embark on relationships with people who aren't really available to commit to us, or we might work to drive people away. Both scenarios involve us being left, and reinforce that life-script belief that we will always be abandoned.

Ciela is a client I worked with in my coaching practice. When she came to me, she was a thirty-eight-year-old woman who was looking to create changes in both her career and personal life, but she felt stuck, bored and unsure of how to change the way her relationships played out:

My pattern in relationships was to embark on wildly intense relationships with 'perfect' men, which would come to a crashing end within a year. This happened several times, and each time I would plunge into a depressed state of self-loathing because at my core I believed I was unlovable.

Life-script work allowed me to identify some of the patterns in my life. Yes, it was true that all of these relationships had ended, but it was also true that I chose men who were damaged and unavailable. Further digging allowed me to reflect on my own childhood — my own father had left my mother and us when I was just three years old. Our relationship after that was inconsistent and I found myself working hard to win his attention and love.

Part of the life script that I'd come to live by was that 'men leave'. I had then unconsciously sought out relationships that would reinforce that belief. When I was really honest with myself, I could see lots of problems in these relationships, which I'd ignored because I was so invested in living out this self-fulfilling prophecy.

Okay, so you've got this and you're recognizing your patterns. 'But, Emmy, what do we dooooo?' I hear you shouting! Well, identifying your patterns is really the first step. It's impossible to change things when we don't know what it is that we're trying to change. Awareness gives us the opportunity to examine all aspects of our life script, and to decide what's useful to us and what isn't.

One tool that I found really helpful was to imagine myself in five or ten years' time, and to write a blurb about what I would be up to then – where I was in my career, where I lived, the kinds of relationships that I had in my life, and so on. I even included lots of pictures in this exercise, because I find visual prompts super-helpful. I then considered what I was holding on to that was unhelpful, and tried to imagine more positive replacements for some of those core beliefs. Essentially, I rewrote my life script based on what I knew as an adult, rather than what I'd unconsciously learned as a small child.

It took me time to retrain my brain to think differently, but with persistence it worked. Even now, if I find some of my old belief systems are triggered, I'm able to spot them and consciously choose not to react in that way. We can change things; we just need to know how.

The wounded child within needs to know that our adult self is able to take care of them. Many of us go through life looking for external things or other people to heal those early wounds. But the truth is that we can learn to heal ourselves, by reassuring our child self that we are able to protect them and keep them safe, to care for them when they're sick, to keep them warm when they're cold, and to feed them when they're hungry. When the child within us begins to feel safe and secure, we are able to let go of some of the destructive coping strategies that we developed in childhood as a way of trying to survive.

Our inner child allows us to express some of the most joyful aspects of life. It allows us to play, sing, dance and create. When you make possible an open dialogue with that part of yourself, give it space and allow it to be heard and seen, then the healing can really begin.

#HealHack

Try to remember some of the things that you loved to do/watch/eat when you were a child. Can you give yourself permission to have some of those things today? Connecting with what we loved when we were a child can feel really comforting as an adult.

Recovery Tool:
How to Self-Care

What is self-care?

Self-care is not a luxury, it is an *essential* survival skill. Self-care gets a lot of stick because I think so many of us are bombarded by images of bubble baths and manicures as references to self-care; and although there is value in those things, frankly I feel it trivializes self-care's importance. True self-care consists of the regular activities and practices that we engage in on a consistent basis to enhance our physical and mental health, in order to restore and maintain balance in our lives.

Lots of us are in the habit of only taking care of ourselves when we're in a crisis, and we'll only stop and take a break when we can feel ourselves close to burning out. Many of us also regard acts of self-care as an indulgence, and so we wouldn't consider taking time for ourselves unless it was a special treat. Yet when we incorporate regular self-care behaviours into our lives, we limit the stresses and pressures that all of us encounter in everyday life.

What are the aims of self-care?

- Managing and reducing anxiety and stress
- Honouring our emotional and spiritual needs
- Nurturing our physical and mental health
- Building intimate relationships with ourselves and others
- Maintaining a consistent sense of internal peace

Developing a self-care plan

For many of my clients, the concept of developing a self-care plan is totally alien. It can be difficult to know where to start, so I've included a list of self-care practices here for you to explore. It is vital that you find which of these really works for you and makes *you* feel good. Consider picking

some practices that could be helpful in maintaining balance day-to-day, and others that might be useful if you find yourself in a crisis.

Once you have developed some strategies for self-care, it can be good to share your plan with people you feel support you. I often talk to friends about how they take care of themselves, and we frequently share book recommendations or experiences and insights we've found helpful.

SELF-CARE MAINTENANCE PRACTICES

- Take a walk in nature
- Get a massage/ pedicure/facial
- Take a break
- Walk your dog – or borrow someone else's!
- Listen to a podcast that you find inspiring
- Sing along to your favourite musical
- Paint a picture or draw
- Write a letter or email to someone that you haven't seen for a long time
- Watch a funny movie (taking the time to really laugh is a personal favourite of mine)

- Take a twenty-four-hour social media break
- Read a story to a child – your own or a friend's (being with children is a wonderful way of being mindful and in the moment)
- Practise a random act of kindness (spending a few minutes chatting to someone you know lives alone or buying a stranger a cup of tea are feel-good acts)
- Curate a playlist of music that makes you feel amazing

- Go to bed early
- Plant some of your own herbs on the windowsill
- Spend some time with someone that inspires you and with whom you can share ideas
- Practise mindfulness (see p. 94)
- Play a sport with a friend
- Go to the movies by yourself
- Write some poetry or seek out a space where you can be creative
- Hug someone you love
- Tell someone you love them

Pick and write down three self-care exercises from the list above (or of your own) that appeal to you. Commit to do them all over the next week, and note down what you found most useful about each.

Step 6: Find Self-Acceptance

The destructive voice will get weaker,
and your perception of yourself will begin to heal.

So many of us look at our physical selves as a way of seeking approval and acceptance within the world. We are taught to scrutinize every flaw and aspire to be in the best physical shape that we possibly can be – and when that's not enough, we are encouraged to fill every crease and inject every line. Do we really believe this is how we're going to find our self-worth? Or have we become conditioned to think that way, and have we unconsciously gone along with it without asking ourselves whether we actually believe in the ideals that we are aiming for?

My own relationship with my body has been a painful one, but it's one that I'm now at peace with. Through my own healing journey I realized that, in order to have a truly compassionate relationship with myself, that would mean embracing and accepting every inch of me. I've starved, cut, punished and pushed my body because, to me, it wasn't good enough . . . not even close.

So whether you're someone who loathes yourself for how you look, or you're someone who has casually

disparaging thoughts about your appearance – or you're somewhere in between – let's keep pushing for something better. Let's aim for a day when we can feel good about what we see in the mirror. Not because we think it's perfect, but because we know that face/body well and it's become a true friend to us.

Self-acceptance over self-hatred

Having a negative attitude towards your own body is without doubt one of the most painful symptoms of living with an unwell voice. Throughout the years that I've worked in this field, I've heard client after client tell me about feeling seriously negative about their body and how they look. When this happens (and because it hurts so badly), they turn to destructive behaviours around food and exercise as a way of feeling better about themselves.

These behaviours don't help though, do they? They masquerade as providing guidance and comfort, when in fact they are fuelled by hatred and negativity, causing us to talk to ourselves with contempt and treat our bodies with loathing.

A dancer called Hope who I worked with for several months had been drawn into precisely this pattern. Her unwell voice dictated such a gruelling schedule with regards to exercise and food that, when we met, Hope was undernourished and injured. The voice had convinced her that she needed to heavily restrict her food to maintain an 'acceptable' physique, but also that she needed to train harder than ever to be successful. Hope had ended up with an injury which nearly finished her career. Fortunately we were able to work on restoring a compassionate connection to food and exercise, but this is a good example of how the unwell voice legitimizes its demands.

How can restricting, hating and punishing our bodies ever really make us feel good? If you're feeling resistant to the idea of accepting yourself as you are, ask yourself this: Have all the years you've been at war with your body actually helped you? I'd bet the answer is a firm 'no'. After all, you're still fighting that same battle, still hating and criticizing your body. The irony is that, all this time, your body has been working tirelessly to protect you and keep you safe.

Acceptance of where we are right now is the first step to overcoming negative body image. Through self-healing, you can develop a respectful relationship with your body – one in which you intuitively take care of it using food, exercise, rest and self-compassion. Your acceptance of you can be born out of a commitment to yourself to live your life to the fullest, nurture a growing sense of self-awareness, heal old wounds and build fulfilling relationships with others.

We cannot fully heal without being willing to fully embrace ALL that we are. Your body is not an ornament; it is a vessel to carry your soul through life, and when you begin to see it as such, you will be able to accept it just as it is.

You might be feeling fearful that, if you work on

accepting yourself, somehow you'll end up letting your-self go. I hear this from clients all the time and it really isn't true; it's just that cruel voice tricking us into thinking that self-acceptance equals getting bigger/more unattract-ive/less lovable, when in fact that's just another unwell thought. Actually, our bodies look their best when they are loved and nurtured, both physically and mentally.

> *'How can I accept my body when*
> *I feel there's so much wrong with it?'*

This is one of the classic stumbling blocks that many people come across: to embark on a journey of self-love, we think that the body needs to be changed before we begin – whereas actually it's the acceptance that comes first. When I talk about self-acceptance, I mean accepting ourselves *as we are today* and loving ourselves *in the present moment*, not *I'll be happy when I've lost ten pounds*.

I'm not saying you have to regard every single aspect of yourself as perfect right now, but it is important to culti-vate a sense that you are good enough just as you are. Like most people, I'm more confident about some parts of my body than others, but I certainly don't berate myself for any of it, and nor do I feel in any way inferior because I have stretch marks and cellulite. If the critical voice arises, I just remind myself that I'm a woman who's living her life and whose body tells a story about that life.

Any scars I have aren't there to be criticized or ridiculed, but merely reflect what I've been through. The jagged line across my knee, for example, pays homage to the time I fell off my bike as a child. The slick line across my abdomen is a reminder of one of the most beautiful days of my life, the day I gave birth to my daughter via Caesarean section. Perspective is everything. If you can begin to shift your perspective and consider what your own 'body story' is, then you can begin to come to a place of acceptance.

When you've suffered trauma, however, it can be easy to confuse feelings of self-loathing towards your body and feelings of self-loathing towards yourself at your core. This is because it might be difficult to understand or process that trauma. What happens then is that the bad feeling gets squeezed through your mind and pops out as a negative thought about your thighs or stomach or arms. Many people will tell me in earnest that if they could just create a physical change, then they'd feel better about themselves. Yet when we go through their history, examining how they've felt about themselves through the years, what always becomes clear is that the core feelings of self-loathing don't actually originate from their feelings towards their body, but are in fact rooted in early trauma.

As a young woman, I restricted my food and worked hard to maintain a certain body type. But I was always surprised when, no matter what the scales said, I still felt unattractive and less than. It felt unfair, as if the goalposts were always shifting. It took a long time for me to realize that I wasn't going to find a sense of peace because of anything external. It had to come from within me.

As I've already said, feeling good about ourselves physically begins with an acceptance of ourselves as we are *today*. But I would like to add this: we must also remember to attend to those core wounds. When we begin to feel better about who we are on the inside, we start to feel good about what we see in the mirror. After all, what makes a person attractive is so often not the way they look but their energy and personality. We've all been in a situation where we've met someone we thought was gorgeous who then became far less attractive once we got to know them! Essentially, the more you like yourself, the more you will appreciate and respect your body – and the more your energy and personality can shine through.

Still feeling doubtful about all this? Let me put it another way. You've most likely spent years trying to feel better about yourself by changing or manipulating your physical appearance – but really, how successful has that quest been? If you can recognize that it hasn't helped, maybe try focusing that energy on healing yourself at the core instead. I think you'd be amazed at the positive impact it could have on your body image.

Negative body triggers

When we have negative body image, it feels as though it is a fact. But have you ever noticed how your perception of yourself can be radically different from one day to the next? So much of how we perceive ourselves physically is dependent on our general mood and how positive we are feeling on a much deeper level.

It's important to treat your negative body-image

thoughts as facets of your unwell voice. At this point in your journey, the aim should be to move away from those behaviours or thoughts that give energy and strength to your unwell voice, and turn towards cultivating loving and positive behaviours instead.

Weighing yourself regularly, pinching flesh on your body, and using social media to flood your phone with other people's supposedly perfect bodies are all triggering behaviours that give your unwell voice ammunition with which to shoot down your self-esteem and self-acceptance.

I know that it can feel impossible to move away from these behaviours straight away, but just take it one day at a time and you really will start to re-create a positive dialogue between yourself and your body.

Here are some tips for understanding and avoiding negative triggers:

- **Avoid the dreaded scales.** Weighing yourself is really self-destructive and, unless your weight needs to be monitored for medical reasons, I would strongly suggest that you stop. That might sound scary right now but I assure you that once you've learned to eat intuitively, and to care for and love your body, it will find a peaceful, stable state and you won't need to monitor how much it weighs.
- **Flip negative self-talk over.** Rather than scrutinizing yourself in the mirror, searching for perceived flaws, or using your phone to take

photos of yourself, make a list of all the things that you're grateful for about your body. Perhaps you're grateful to have your ears to listen to music or your eyes to read a book. Start with the basics and take it from there – it's amazing when the energy starts to shift in a more positive direction!

- **Beware of social media.** We are constantly bombarded by images of what we're 'supposed' to look like. Social media can be a good and a bad thing, and it's important to use it wisely. It can be damaging to follow people and accounts that are promoting restrictive behaviours or lifestyle choices (an obsession with health, thinness or exercise, for example), but it can be uplifting and inspiring to follow those who challenge a lot of society's ideas about how women should behave and look.

- **Remember that negativity is contagious.** When I decided that I wanted to change my life, I realized that I had to change who I spent my time with and what I spent my time talking about. It's draining to spend time with people who are focused on sharing a negative view of themselves or are fixated on negative talk, and that negativity can also be infectious. Don't worry – I'm not saying you have to completely ditch your friends or any loved ones who are facing a similar struggle, but you do need to set some boundaries around topics of conversation that are potentially triggering.

Try to accept that today you are a work in progress. Adopting new patterns of thinking takes time, but you can and you will change how you see yourself. You *can* choose to try to embrace all parts of yourself, even those that seem 'imperfect' to you.

Daily Affirmations to Cultivate Self-Acceptance

- *I am worthy of love and respect.*
- *I accept my body today.*
- *My body deserves to be nourished.*
- *I forgive myself.*
- *I use food to nurture my body and my soul.*
- *I move my body because I enjoy it.*
- *My body is a vessel that I take care of.*

Let's talk about food

So few of us have a relationship with food where we are able to eat freely and intuitively, without guilt or shame. A 'normal' and healthy relationship with food has become corrupted by damaging messages in the media, tedious cultural demands that insist we look and behave in a certain way, and an unrelenting shame about our basic needs and desires: we should not feel hunger, we should not desire, we should not want. I regularly see depictions of women in the media who are underweight, and in films women are rarely shown eating. These seemingly casual depictions constantly influence our choices and how we believe we will be viewed. Even for those of us who think we have a good relationship with food, there is often still room for improvement.

What is intuitive eating?

Intuitive eating is when we tune in to our body's physical cues and trust them to let us know what we want and need at any given time. It is about letting go of *any* rules around food – there are no diets, no restrictive patterns or supposedly 'healthy' eating plans. Intuitive eating is about learning that you are the person who knows best what your body needs and when.

When you're in the early stages of doing this work and you come to realize that your relationship with food has been controlled by your unwell voice, it can be both difficult and frightening to suddenly start listening to – and trusting – your body. That's why intuitive eating might be something that you have to work slowly towards.

It can take time for regular hunger and fullness cues to return, and it may also take a while for you to recognize them, particularly if you've suffered with disordered eating patterns for a long time. Learning to identify and trust these cues is all part of the healing process.

If you decide to begin exploring intuitive eating, always be mindful of your unwell voice and its readiness to manipulate you as you deviate from the safety of old restrictive belief systems. The unwell voice will be ready to challenge you each time you try to make a choice based on what you feel you want and need. Be prepared for comments like 'You don't need that cake, do you?' or 'She's not eating that, you need to have what she's having' or 'You can only eat that if you work out later'.

The key thing here is to manage your expectations and take your time. Making peace with food and your body can be emotional, but food is really not your enemy, I promise – its only job is to energize you and make you feel good!

Is all emotional eating bad?

Nope! The term 'emotional eating' has extremely negative connotations for most people, largely because it's highly misunderstood. The role that food has in society is not solely about nutrition and maintaining optimum physical health; it also has emotional benefits too.

Developing a positive emotional relationship with food is something to work towards, and it exists in a world where you are free from using food as a destructive and punishing tool for coping. It's all possible.

Many people feel apprehensive of connecting any emotional pleasure whatsoever with food. They're afraid that doing so will become unhealthy and fuel destructive behaviours. But when we achieve a respectful relationship between our bodies, minds and food, we can welcome that connection.

Negative emotional eating might look like:

- *I'm feeling lonely and a little sad and I want to block out all the loneliness and sadness, just to push it down with biscuits until I can't feel anything any more except the fullness in my stomach.*
- *I'm feeling stressed with work and responsibilities and I wish I could just feel less overwhelmed. I buy a huge 99 ice cream on my lunch break and then I feel so guilty for eating it that I think I'm a failure and may as well buy another. Then I feel even more of a failure and my mood drops until I can't face going back to work or seeing anyone.*
- *I'm unwell with the flu and fed up. Because I feel so unproductive, I feel like I don't deserve to eat, so I ignore my craving for my mother's chicken soup, which used to make me feel so cared for when I was sick as a child.*

Positive emotional eating might look like:

- *I'm feeling lonely and a little sad, so I'm craving food that is warm and comforting to my body. I eat this food as a way of nurturing and caring for myself because my body feels content and satisfied when I've finished my meal.*
- *I'm feeling stressed with work and responsibilities and am longing for a sense of childlike freedom. I buy a huge 99 ice cream on my lunch break and walk through the park. I'm not hungry at all but I want the ice cream to satisfy a craving for pleasure and needing to connect to my child self. I feel good and comforted afterwards.*

- *I'm unwell with the flu and I'm fed up. I want my mother's chicken soup because just the smell of it makes me feel cared for and helps boost my wellbeing.*

What is mindfulness and how can it help us find self-acceptance?

Have you ever had the experience of 'waking up' (or 'coming to') in the middle of a conversation, only to realize that you have no idea what's just been said? Instead of listening, you've been completely absorbed by your ruminations, reliving a past event in your mind or thinking about the future? Everybody does this occasionally, but when it's a frequent occurrence it can really interrupt our ability to connect with each other and the world around us. I'd even go so far as to say that it can disconnect us from what it means to be truly alive, since so much of our joy as human beings comes when we are fully engaged in what we are doing *right now*.

Mindfulness is essentially the opposite of the experience I mentioned above. It's a way of living and an attitude to life that revolves around developing your sense of self-awareness (whatever is going on in your thoughts and feelings) *in the present moment*. Only when we develop awareness do we have any hope of being able to choose how we react to what life throws at us. Living an empowered life is all about learning how to react in new, healthier ways to your thoughts and feelings, hence mindfulness is something we practise and cultivate in the clinic.

94

What is mindfulness *not*?

Contrary to what many people assume, mindfulness is *not* about trying to control your thinking, but rather noticing what you're thinking about. When we observe thoughts as mere thoughts we automatically give ourselves more opportunity to 'come back' and refocus our attention on whatever is happening in the here and now, and then choose if we want to react.

For example, in the early days of my own self-healing, I would 'name it' (internally) when I heard myself have an unwell thought. I would say to myself, *That's an unwell thought; I can let that go.* It was very much a conscious process initially, but with practice and persistence it became easier and easier.

Why is developing mindfulness so important?

What usually happens during this self-healing journey, as people begin to identify their unwell voice, is that they notice a constant critical train of thought passing through their minds. Historically we've just been experiencing all of these self-destructive thoughts and feelings and simply absorbing them. Once absorbed, those thoughts and feelings have probably then been manifesting in the way that we treat ourselves and how we live our lives.

One of the first stages of the healing process is developing an internal dialogue so that you can actually begin to interact with this unwell voice. As I've said before, trying to ignore the voice or distract yourself from it can make it even louder (until, eventually, you give in to it in order to get some peace). I promise neither of those tactics will work, and even if you manage to sidestep disordered and destructive behaviours, your unwell voice will still attack you.

There is a way through this stuff, however. The more you practise mindfulness, the more you can begin to dilute the power of the unwell voice, observing it merely as the sounds of unwell thoughts. Let me say that again, because it's important . . . These are just unwell thoughts. Just. Unwell. Thoughts.

I know that might seem a little far-fetched right now. But all you need do at this point is trust me that practising mindfulness is making a commitment to living fully – to getting the most out of your life on a daily or even hourly basis. Yes, it can be hard when you're experiencing difficult thoughts or feelings, and yes, it might seem easier to distract yourself from them than it is to simply observe and sit with them. But trust me, like I said: regular and continued mindfulness practice can and will enable you to sit with your negative thoughts, observing them with compassion for yourself until they disperse.

A nice way of starting this process, like all things, is by being curious and kind to yourself. Begin by trying to become fully conscious whenever you are walking anywhere. Notice where your mind takes you and be curious about your responses to the constant thoughts that you have firing off in your brain. Do you find that a single thought hijacks your entire experience? Do you get swept up in what a friend of mine describes as 'incessant monkey chatter'? Get to know yourself and give yourself permission to 'observe' your mind, rather than get drawn into responding to each thought.

What should you do when you notice an unwell thought?

I've explained why I don't want you to ignore your unwell voice, and obviously I don't want you to act on it. Instead, I want you to counter it with a compassionate and kind affirmation. If you have a thought that tells you that you are not good enough, try responding with *I am good enough* and *I can do this*. When that unwell voice says something like 'Nobody likes you, so don't bother going to that party', try responding with *I am worthy* and *I choose to be kind and compassionate to myself today*.

The thing about the unwell voice is that it creates a problem and then offers a solution. For example, it might tell you, 'You can't go out for dinner and see your friends because if you do, then you can't restrict your food intake as much as you'd like.' Then that same voice offers a solution: 'Okay, go out for dinner, but just make sure you diet for the rest of the week.'

It can be hard to challenge this voice, however unhealthy its suggestions. Many of us feel frightened about stepping away from our unwell voice because it has seemed to help us cope with difficult situations in the past. But, actually, the unwell voice is responsible for creating the problem in the first place – for example, the anxiety and fear around having to socialize in a new setting. If we buy into that problem, and the suggestions that come from our unwell voice, we don't have a real solution – we just perpetuate the issue and maintain the whole painful self-destructive cycle. Introducing a kind and compassionate voice that soothes and reassures us is what we want to achieve.

I understand if this sounds strange. It can feel really alien when you first start challenging your unwell voice and thoughts in this way (developing an internal dialogue and having battles inside your head). But, so long as you persist, I can promise that the destructive voice will get weaker – and your perception of yourself will begin to heal.

Commit to a happier self

Today, you have a choice. You can choose to spend the rest of your life being at war with your physical self – starving it, punishing it and shaming yourself – or you can choose to accept yourself today. Embrace your body for the gifts that it has bestowed upon you, and use it to embrace your experience of being human.

In order to have a nurturing and compassionate relationship with ourselves, we must accept ourselves for who we are today. From this point on, we can truly begin to heal.

#HealHack

The only kind of 'cleanse' that I have ever endorsed is a social media one. Get on your feed and unfollow anyone or anything that doesn't support your intention to be your most loved self. It feels good!

Recovery Tool: Body Image
Healing Meditation

If you've been living with negative body image then you'll have spent a huge amount of time battling with the unwell voice inside your head that's constantly attacking you and flooding your mind with disparaging thoughts. Experiencing this can be damaging and draining.

This meditation is designed to support you and help you begin to heal your body image. There are no rules about how you should meditate, or on how specifically

you should reflect on your experience – though you might find it helpful to record yourself reading this meditation out loud so you can use it as a guide, or download it here: https://emmybrunner.com/body-image-healing-meditation.

If you feel overwhelmed or as though you'd like to stop at any time, please feel free to revisit this when you're feeling stronger. The process of healing should be gentle and compassionate, so be mindful not to place excessively high expectations on yourself. You may also find that once you've finished this meditation you feel especially vulnerable and in need of some comfort, so think about lining up some self-care activities or tools now that you can use afterwards.

Beginning now, have a seat on the floor and make yourself comfortable. Take a few minutes to consider the ways in which your body has been serving you and what you might be grateful for.

Gratitude can be very simple indeed. Try to focus on how your body functions as opposed to how it looks, and ask: what does your body do that you feel grateful for? You may feel pleased that you have legs that allow you to walk, a heart that continues to beat. Or you may feel grateful that you can enjoy lovely smells and hear the sound of birds singing in spring. Whatever makes you feel blessed, that's enough.

Close your eyes gently – or, if this feels like too much, allow your gaze to rest on the floor. Focus your attention on your breath, the soft rise and fall of your chest, the air travelling in and out of your body. Be mindful that you don't try to control this process, and instead attempt to just let go and simply witness whatever is happening. Allow yourself to feel the ground beneath you and notice the support of your body as it rests in this position. Become aware of any feelings or sensations that begin to arise within you. Consider any smells that you recognize, the temperature of the air around you and any sounds that you can hear.

Let all of this wash over you as you simply sit still in each moment. Now focus your attention again on your breath and the temperature of the air as it enters and leaves your body. Breathe in and out, in and out. Imagine for a moment that your breath has healing powers. See yourself as inhaling a cleansing and rejuvenating breath, and then exhaling tension, toxins and negativity out of your body. Imagine a warmth beginning in your toes and feet, and allow that warmth to feel comforting and calm. Let that warm relaxation spread across your feet, up to your ankles and calves, and slowly start to let it flow up through your body, relaxing you more and more as it goes.

Next, conjure a sense of your body healing from physical and emotional wounds. Connect with a sense of gratitude for your ability to care for and nurture yourself. Focus now on any tension that exists within your body. This could be small and subtle or it could be something major or more long-term – just focus on anything that you wish to heal, and hold that in your mind for now.

Now direct your attention to the specific location in your body where this particular problem is present. You might want to associate this part of your body with a dark shadow, and then see the warmth flowing through you as a kind of healing light. See that healing light move towards your more shadowy areas, casting a glow over them. See the light aiding your body's healing process, boosting your immune system, ridding your body of pain, toxins and any discomfort. Return your focus to your healing breath again – and, as you exhale, see your body expelling the dark shadows within.

Connect once more with that overwhelming sense of gratitude for your body, and recognize it as a gift to be loved and nurtured. Breathe in healing; breathe out tension and stress. Allow the light within your body to continue to diminish the darkness, and see that darkness getting smaller and smaller and smaller.

Notice any feelings of peace and confidence in your body and in your ability to love and nurture your physical self.

Breathe in and out as you return your focus to the room; and slowly, whenever you're ready, open your eyes.

Well done. Now you can continue with your day knowing that you can accelerate your healing with this meditation whenever you so choose.

Step 7: Believe That You Can and Will Recover

If we believe that we are confident, inspired, creative and successful people, then our external lives reflect that.

The greatest shifts that I've ever made in my life have been when I started to believe that what I wanted was actually possible. The unwell voice had really battered me over the years, and in the beginning I struggled to imagine a different kind of life for myself. Over time, I read a lot about how what we actually believe about ourselves becomes our reality. So I started to ask myself . . . surely that must also be true for mental health and recovery? What if I decided to believe I could heal, and become exactly who I chose to be?

I took a risk, I believed I could and I did. How much faith and belief do you have in your ability to change and create the life that you want? Now is the time. This is your opportunity to connect with your greatest potential and become inspired.

Can we really change?

One of the biggest myths surrounding mental illness is that nobody ever wholly recovers, and that people can merely learn to manage their symptoms better.

When people first come into my clinic, they talk in depth about feelings of despair and hopelessness. I think much of this comes from the fear that they are going to have to live with their soul-destroying shame and pain forever.

This isn't true. However, cultivating faith in recovery is one of the biggest challenges for sufferers. This is also the case for those of us who, although we may not be in a state of crisis or have been diagnosed with a particular condition, also can't imagine living without that critical voice inside our heads, and find it impossible to believe that things really can change.

My response to anyone feeling this way is always the same: What if you're wrong? What if things *can* change? What if it *is* possible for you to heal?

I know from my own journey that healing is absolutely possible, but that we have to believe it's possible if we are going to achieve it. To put it another way: doubting that you can fully recover from your internal wounds is one of the biggest obstacles to getting over them completely. I accepted that 'my way' of living ultimately wasn't working for me, and I decided that I had nothing to lose by putting faith into something else. I practised believing, even when I didn't feel I had any real conviction in it.

The recovery tools throughout this book will help you
to create shifts that will fuel your belief that you can do
this . . . and that is exactly what they were designed to do.

And you can. You really can change your world if you
want to.

Change your thoughts, change your world

Like many people, I was raised to make choices based on
fear, scarcity and duty. I never really hoped for or aspired
to much in life, because I didn't think anything truly great
was possible for me and I was too afraid to try.

I spent my late teens and early twenties dealing with the consequences of those fear-fuelled choices. I felt scared of everything, and didn't or couldn't trust anyone. I didn't know how. I played very small in my career, had multiple abusive relationships and avoided intimacy with anyone. Later, I began to explore different spiritual teachings and came to understand that my thoughts and beliefs had actually created my reality. I realized that if I wanted my environment to change, I needed to change my perspective on life.

Adopting positivity has been one of the greatest things I've ever done for myself. I believe that how we choose to start each new day dictates precisely the kind of day that we then have. Choosing to maintain a positive outlook and feeling hopeful about what the day may hold will change the day itself. On the other hand, ruminating, worrying and feeling anxious is the best way to line up further challenges.

Both options are available to all of us, and it's important to remind ourselves that we have a choice about which path we go down. That way, we can empower ourselves to take action about anything we're not happy about. The 'letting go' can be scary, but when we do just that and begin to nurture a compassionate relationship with ourselves, we are inspired to make choices that support that view.

So much of this process is about 'waking up'. We spend 95 per cent of our lives running on autopilot and acting and reacting without being fully present. When we go about our days, we are able to get to work and perform daily tasks without having to really 'think' about what we're doing. We are often thinking about other things entirely: the fight we had with our partner, what we are going to make for dinner, or a television programme we just watched. Yet our subconscious mind is still working, and part of the process of healing is when we become conscious and mindful of how often we are in this distracted state.

When we are not consciously present in our own lives, we become passive bystanders – even though we are creating our reality with our thoughts and actions. When we become conscious, we engage in our lives with intention and purpose – and from this platform we become the creator of our reality.

If we want to change, then we have to become conscious of our subconscious behaviour. As we begin to observe our own patterns and how we act, we give ourselves the opportunity to change and to make new choices; we can't do this when we are disconnected and disengaged.

Whenever I sense dissatisfaction with any area of my life, I remind myself that if I want to change something, then I need to change how I'm thinking about it. When I had my first child I was frantically trying to manage my business and look after my daughter with very little support. I was a single parent and would become seriously overwhelmed on a day-to-day basis. So I sat myself down one day and asked myself whether life was working for me. The answer was clearly 'no'. But I also realized that I had a lot more control over how I was feeling than I'd thought. I needed to mark out clear times for work and for mothering, and I needed to find a support system that worked for me. By doing less work, I was actually able to be more productive. I was also able to be fully present when I was with my daughter, and that changed everything for me.

I've since developed this further, and now prioritize my own self-care above anything else – because I realized that if I want to be good at anything, I have to take care of myself and be as kind to myself as possible. My self-care routine is now a big part of the day-to-day rhythm of my life. I meditate, I journal and I make time for myself. I know for certain that focusing on my own wellbeing has facilitated me to have a more successful career and be a more available parent.

Embracing a positive perspective has altered my world dramatically, and encouraging others to do the same has become an integral part of the work that I do in my clinic. If we want to be more joyful and to have more love in our lives, then we must begin with the most important relationship of all – our relationship with ourselves. I encourage the people I work with to become their own best friends and to always have their own backs.

We are all able to choose to support our desires rather than sabotage them. It's just about deciding to think that way. I believe that, for each of us, our world reflects our internal belief system. What we believe about ourselves becomes a self-fulfilling prophecy. If we are confident, inspired, creative and successful people, then our external lives will reflect that. Equally, if we are lacking in confidence and self-esteem or we are full of self-loathing, then, just as surely, our lives reflect that.

Here are some examples of how we unconsciously

reinforce our core beliefs about ourselves with our own behaviour:

Thought: I am unattractive to others.
Behaviour: I avoid social occasions because I feel ashamed of how I look.
Consequence 1: I'm less likely to meet anyone, because I don't have the confidence or opportunity to meet new people.
Consequence 2: Further social isolation and a lowered sense of self-worth.
Core belief is reinforced → I'm unattractive

Thought: I am stupid.
Behaviour: I don't aspire to achieve, or seek new opportunities, because I don't think I'm capable.
Consequence 1: I stay in menial roles that I find unfulfilling.
Consequence 2: I give up on new challenges because I have no confidence in my abilities.
Core belief is reinforced → I am stupid.

Thought: I am always sick.
Behaviour: I obsessively think about illness and my health.
Consequence 1: I am highly anxious, and worry constantly about being ill.
Consequence 2: I become physically unwell because I am constantly worrying and anxious.
Core belief is reinforced → I am always sick.

Thought: I am unlovable.

Behaviour: I seek out relationships with abusive partners, because I don't think I'm deserving of love.

Consequence 1: I am repeatedly abused, neglected or hurt.

Consequence 2: Ultimately these partners reject me. Nobody wants me.

Core belief is reinforced → I am unlovable.

We talk about the law of attraction a lot in my clinic, and I regularly explain how recovery is all about focusing on what you want – as opposed to what you don't want. The unwell voice is very strong because it is exercised so frequently; it's always there in the background, criticizing every perceived flaw and finding fault in everything that you do. By continually thinking about the negative aspects of ourselves, we feel dragged down and miserable. Conversely, when we focus our intention on what we want, we feel better.

It's important to note here that many people will say that they are constantly focused on wanting the perfect body, life or career, but this still comes from a negative thought – that what they already have is not good enough. We can reframe this as: 'I am grateful for X, and I am working to develop these areas of my life.'

I myself am working towards developing my clinic and the ways that we work with people; but that's not about striving for perfection, it's about a willingness to grow and develop – and that energy feels very different.

I understand that it's hard to start thinking differently, I'm not denying that. Sometimes it can feel like wading through mud. But it's vital to remember that you didn't always feel this way. Just look at a toddler examining themselves in the mirror – you'll notice their curiosity and joy when they see their own reflection. It is only the external interventions and influences that corrupt this enchanting view – a view that all of us had of ourselves once.

My client Mary is someone who had lost that view of herself and was striving from milestone to milestone that others had set for her. She thought she was happy, but something didn't feel quite right:

My healing journey has crept up on me like a happy accident. I was that person that scoffed at the idea of therapy, thought that anyone that meditated was a mental hippy and sat in judgement on anyone that went on any kind of retreat or self-help course. I also had an ego the size of a small country and I'd managed to convince myself that I was smashing it in pretty much every area of my life. I had the great job, the gorgeous flat, the friends and the hot boyfriend. It was only when I got engaged that my well-established facade began to crumble. I couldn't continue to ignore who I was or what I wanted. I didn't marry him; I just couldn't 'force' that next step.

Reluctantly, I went along with a friend to hear a 'mental hippy' talking about how to leverage your mental health for the creative good. The thing was, this woman wasn't a mental hippy; she was bright, accomplished and appeared on some level to have it together. She talked about how unprocessed trauma dictates the choices that we make as adults, and that simple insight hit me so hard that

I couldn't move. Suddenly everything in my life began to make sense. I connected for the first time with a deep and cavernous sense of loneliness and realized that I was living a life meant for someone else. I had made choices based on what I believed my family and society wanted for me. I had approached life like a series of checklists and had never stopped to ask myself who I was or what I wanted. I left that lecture and decided that I would change my life.

I spent the next six months seeking out talks, books and experiences that could help me foster a greater connection with who I really was. It was the most challenging and illuminating experience that I've ever had. I came to realize that if I didn't nurture the relationship that I had with myself, then I would never have anything to offer anyone else. I connected with a sense of something far greater than myself and something that I still today don't have the language to articulate, but it's something that has given me a faith that I never thought was possible. It's not religious, it's not flighty or woo-woo . . . it's grounded and strong and I feel anchored to something for the first time in my life.

Be curious about who you are – you never know what you may find.

How many of us have pursued one thing even though a voice deep inside us told us not to? The answer is *all of us*. As we progress through the journey of life, we are all able to look back with insight and wisdom, and recognize, for example, when we chose the wrong partner even though our intuition told us they were trouble. We can reflect and see that we didn't apply for that job because we didn't think we were capable, even though our intuition was shouting 'Do it!' Understanding this is all part of the journey. We make mistakes, naturally, but we need to learn from them rather than going into our later years still ignoring our well voice, which has been there all along trying to steer us towards the light.

Be brave: Invest your energies in love and gratitude

The universe is a wondrous and beautiful place, and the more we invest in creating a life that we feel truly excited and inspired by, the more likely it is that we will see that life form around us. We can manifest anything into our lives if we believe it is possible, including creating a more nurturing and compassionate relationship with ourselves.

If you notice that you are feeling bogged down by negative thoughts or a lack of faith, get out your vision board (see pp. 56–9), write down your affirmations, call a friend who is inspiring or perform your favourite mood shifter (see pp. 155–9) – anything to get yourself buzzing on a frequency of love and abundance once again.

As you begin to be able to observe your thoughts, you will come to see that your emotions are shifting constantly throughout your day. As you increase your own self-awareness, you will no longer be a slave to your emotions as they flux and change; you will be able to actively choose what emotions you invest your energy and focus in, and will become the master of your own life.

If you are reading this and feeling paralysed by depression and anxiety, then I want to speak straight to you now: I see you, I know that pain and this is a process. You don't need to be able to climb the mountain today; you just need to take a first step. This is a practice that takes time, commitment and patience, so just keep faith and know that the changes will come in time.

It's okay to feel afraid

Sometimes we can feel entirely paralysed by fear. When we are scared, we focus on the cause of our fear, over and over again. As we do this, the subject of our fear grows and grows and grows until it is so strong that we simply feel overwhelmed.

By focusing on something positive, we begin to give strength to something better — some other part of ourselves that longs to feel hopeful and inspired.

For example, we may think, *I'm scared that I'm going to be alone forever. I'm alone because I'm unattractive and boring. I'm getting older and no one wants me. I'll never have children. I'm so overwhelmed I can't do this any more.*

But this can become: *I'm scared that I'm going to be alone forever. I recognize that this is a thought based in fear. I'm going to be really kind to myself today because I'm feeling a little vulnerable.*

As you heal and foster a greater sense of self-worth, you will find it increasingly easy to manifest these positive life shifts.

Fear may fill our world, but it doesn't have to fill our hearts. Just because this may be the way that you have lived your life up until now, it doesn't mean that you can't change that. Rewriting your life script (all those ideas you used to have about your limitations; all the negative messages you picked up during your upbringing; all your historic beliefs about the way life *is*) is a courageous and life-affirming act. *I am brave* is one of my favourite meditation mantras. Just waking up in the morning and saying that to yourself can change the whole tone of your day.

If you find that you are having a hard day, or things don't seem like they're going right, just remember that setbacks in life don't necessarily mean that you're not on the right track. Life's challenges are opportunities for self-reflection and growth, and some of the most difficult experiences that we are faced with are wonderful opportunities to learn. When we don't define ourselves by external experiences, we will no longer find that they send us into a spiral of chaos and uncertainty, and we are able to remain grounded and present.

I have run my own business for fifteen years, which has been both immensely challenging and rewarding. I was never trained in any sort of business management and I've made lots of mistakes. Now when things don't 'flow' I trust that they are not meant to be, and I look back on past 'failures' as opportunities to gain insight. I don't attribute difficult events to a personal flaw; I am resilient and inspired by change, but that shift has come by schooling myself in exactly the kind of thinking that I'm offering to you here.

Deciding to allow your well voice to guide you can seem scary, because allowing fear to guide your choices is so familiar to you. But I'll say it again – *be brave*. The more you trust in yourself and your inner guide, the more empowered you'll become. To put your faith in something unseen and unknown can feel scary, but I urge you to take that risk, to turn to love and away from fear. You've never seen love and you can't touch love, yet you believe in it, don't you? You can hold love in your heart and you can feel its presence even though it's intangible and invisible. So put your energy and faith in love, and accept the presence of fear but stop fighting it – it's a waste of precious energy. Believe in yourself, follow your heart, listen to your inner guidance and turn inwards for the answers.

So many of my clients have told me that they cannot 'trust' themselves. They look back on a life littered with what they perceive to be poor choices that they regret, and say that this makes it impossible to have faith. The truth is that none of them were listening to their well voice and that is why they made poor choices, as they didn't prioritize their own needs or cultivate a voice to articulate those needs.

This process of turning inwards and strengthening a well voice will allow you to trust yourself, and by investing some faith in this process and yourself you will find that you will come to trust your decisions, both big and small, and you'll be willing to take risks. You will no longer be terrified of failure or making mistakes, because your sense of self will not be dependent on external things like your job or relationship. If these things are not going well at that moment in time, it doesn't mean that you are a bad person.

When you have been surrounded by negative thoughts, negative behaviours and negative consequences, it's easy to become stuck in a rut. Now is the time to shift your thoughts and emotions onto something positive, and begin to draw a sense of joy and greatness towards yourself. For those of you who are still feeling scared and trepidatious, I'd like to invite you to take a chance.

As I always say, 'Come on in, the water's lovely.'

Letting go

'Letting go' was a phrase that I heard a lot in my own healing journey, and at the time I couldn't begin to imagine how important and transformative it would be. For years I was tied up in this illusion that I was able to control everything around me. I worked tirelessly to force the outcomes that I wanted and worked myself to the bone to try to make sure that life goals happened on my timeline.

I was brought up to believe that if you want to succeed, you should work as hard as possible – and I took that literally. I was growing my clinic at the time and had very little support around me, but I found it impossible to trust my own intuition and so I was constantly seeking approval and validation around my business decisions and my relationship choices, from family members and friends. I was frequently left feeling frustrated, confused, exhausted and incredibly stressed.

Letting go was about surrendering to the idea that the universe had a far better idea of what was meant for me than I did. I realized that trying to control everything had not created wonderful opportunities for me – in fact the opposite was true, and I was stifled and stuck. Work felt like a slog, and it was quickly becoming a life that I didn't want for myself and my daughter. I decided that by handing the control back to the universe and letting go, I was giving myself permission to go with the tide and to trust that what was meant for me wouldn't pass me by. I stopped trying to control what others were doing and relaxed.

Previously I'd had my head down working so hard that I couldn't see where I was going. By looking up I started to really see how I could develop and grow my business, and I noticed opportunities that I had been blind to before.

So many of us get caught in a codependent cycle of trying to control our own experiences and the behaviours of those we have relationships with. For those of you who haven't heard of codependency, I define this as 'a dependent and dysfunctional state where we sacrifice our own needs in order to prioritize the needs of others'.

When we consider what being 'controlling' in a relationship means, I think that many of us imagine an abusive significant other who won't allow their partner to wear what they want, have their own friends, etc. But what I came to learn on my healing journey was that I had many codependent behaviours which were based on trying to avoid conflict and volatile situations.

Examples of codependent behaviours include:

- Taking responsibility for someone else's actions.
- Going above and beyond at our job or at home to earn approval.

- Feeling obligated to do things for others without considering our own needs.
- Enabling someone to take advantage of our time or kindness, etc.
- Putting other people's needs ahead of our own.
- Covering up to protect others from facing the consequences of their poor choices.
- Trying to change other people and solve their problems.
- Manipulating others in order to avoid conflict or other challenging situations.
- Neglecting our own needs in the process of caring for someone who doesn't want to care for themselves.

Choosing to let go and stop controlling allows us space to move away from these codependent behaviours and to consciously consider what is motivating our decisions. Instead of making choices based on what other people might think and need, we begin to listen to and honour our *own* needs. When we begin to treat ourselves with this level of respect, we are also communicating something to the world about what we feel we need and deserve. In letting go, we release all doubt, worry and fear about the future, because we are able to trust in something greater than ourselves. In doing so, we create space for new opportunities and relationships, and find peace.

You are worthy of healing because you exist. Your self-doubt and shame may be standing in the way of manifesting your own unique gifts, but they're there nonetheless. Life is no longer going to be just about surviving; it is going to be about nurturing and loving yourself on a daily basis.

#HealHack

Write down three areas of your life where you feel that you are at your most controlling. Then write down three affirmative statements about how you are going to let control of these areas go! You've got this!

Step 8: Tackling Anxiety and Worry

Compassion and kindness are so often the keys to resolving or healing conflict, both within ourselves and externally.

Anxiety not only fuels further anxious thoughts; it can also cause physical reactions. The body responds to anxiety by releasing cortisol and other stress hormones, and these can lead to a range of distressing and unpleasant symptoms.

Living with anxiety can be a lonely and isolating experience. As a previous client once explained, 'You cannot see my pain – people don't understand anxiety, and they too often think willpower can make it go away and that I can somehow "pull myself together".'

Are we all suffering from anxiety disorders?

I don't think that I've ever assessed a client who didn't report feeling anxious. Some of them suffered a debilitating anxiety that affected all areas of their life, whereas for others the experience of anxiety was more like a persistent annoying buzzing around their head that simply followed them throughout their day.

Some of those clients had official diagnoses for their symptoms, such as generalized anxiety disorder or obsessive-compulsive disorder, but many just accepted their anxiety symptoms as part of who they were. The one thing I found consistent is that these people didn't realize that as well as seeking professional advice, they had the power to contribute to resolving their own symptoms. So often when people start to feel anxious, they immediately try to identify the cause of their anxiety, searching around in their mind for all the things they might be worried about and then setting to work, trying to eliminate or resolve those issues. Yet anxiety isn't necessarily a response to an actual event or problem – and so when you've resolved the issue or the cause of your anxiety has diminished, your anxiety will just find another thing to focus on. That's why many sufferers describe feeling anxious a lot, without even having any specific thing to worry about; the anxiety sits within the body and feels impossible to shift. Like I said earlier, anxiety just *exists*.

If you're suffering with anxiety then you will know that it can use anything to justify its presence: for instance, *I'm really anxious because I have an interview tomorrow*, or *I'm really anxious because I look fat*. This then draws the sufferer in to trying to resolve the anxiety by responding to the perceived problem: *I won't go to that interview and then I won't be anxious*, or *I'll lose weight and then I won't feel anxious about feeling fat*.

The anxiety will seemingly reward the sufferer by temporarily alleviating the intensity of the feeling; but, sure enough, that anxiety will return shortly after, stronger than ever. As anyone with anxiety knows, the goalposts are always shifting – the unwell voice isn't satisfied for long – so we need to find a better, more sustainable way of soothing our anxiety.

My client Tuesday turned her anxiety into art. Her story shows how anxiety can appear at any time, over seemingly nothing much at all:

I feel fortunate in that I had one of those lightbulb, 'one day I'll share this as an anecdote on Graham Norton's show' moments in realizing I had a problem with anxiety. It formed the catalyst for a short film I made about my experiences with anxiety, and was a moment of intense clarity and relief for me.

I was stood in a queue in the bank and I suddenly remembered I needed to buy toilet roll. My stomach flipped, I went to leave the queue to buy said toilet roll, then realized I couldn't as I had to stay in the bank. I made a panicky reminder note in my phone and generally had a reaction that would be more justified if I'd realized I'd left the hair straighteners on and trapped the cat in the same room.

It wasn't an overly stressful day, I wasn't running around rushed with a million things I needed to do. I realized I just had a constant feeling of panic. All the time. That was punctuated by stomach flips – and unfortunately I hadn't noticed it, ever. But on this unremarkable day doing unremarkable life admin, something clicked.

It was almost laughable to me at the time. The clarity I felt was a stark contrast to the slightly blurry, out-of-focus way I had been going about my life. I realized something was 'off' in the way I was living day-to-day. That the constant, almost-invisible dread swirling in my stomach wasn't normal.

I felt relieved. I made an appointment to see my doctor, I received full marks on some multiple-choice anxiety questionnaire fired off to me by the doctor and I was prescribed medication.

It was the beginning and a very crucial moment in my recovery, which I'm utterly grateful for. Medication helped, but it wasn't the full solution. The most significant part of my journey was gently unpacking the origins of these destructive feelings that had become so familiar. I came to realize the underlying issues contributing to my anxious thoughts and feelings. It's deep and can go way back to childhood. I've sometimes felt like I've opened Pandora's box and wished I could go back to slam it shut. Ignorance is bliss. But I've been reassured this is not the answer. And although it's been painful and difficult at times, I know I'm in a stronger position now than if I hadn't.

A recurring theme for me was acknowledging my unwell voice. I didn't even know there was another type of voice. One softer and gentler. I'd argue with my therapist that the critical voice protects, motivates or looks after me in some ways, but I soon learned that this was my clever little unwell voice still doing the talking and me doing the listening. An endless endeavour to protect its reign by proving its worth.

You don't fight a critical voice, you nurture and encourage your kind and compassionate voice. I didn't even realize I had one. Eventually I started to hear mine. At first I thought it was weak, there to throw me off track, kill my ambitions in life and turn me into a crystal-wearing sap. You can't achieve anything worthwhile with that soft, mushy voice as your soundtrack, *I incorrectly thought. But slowly I acknowledged and strengthened it. I learned that approaching things with anxiety and fear as motivators will ultimately fail. And my experiences in life so far had been proof of this. Now, when I'm having my weaker moments, when I feel like my anxiety is winning again, I step back and try to be silent – and more often than not what's causing me dread, depleting my energy and soul, is my critical voice. It has taken centre stage and trampled all over my kinder, compassionate voice.*

Showing kindness towards myself and spending time with kind people are some of the ways I boost my compassionate voice. Spending time on my own helps too. I occasionally forget this and have to remind myself. Mid-recovery I would be angry at myself when I let the unwell voice win and take over, and for allowing myself to spend time with negative people and partaking in destructive behaviour or toxic patterns. But I soon discovered this was also the same voice, looking for very clever and covert ways to make me feel bad. So sneaky! Now when I realize I'm taking direction from an unwell voice, I endeavour to meet this with kindness and compassion.

I was surprised that dealing with my anxiety wasn't the main focus in therapy. It became the background extra rather than the leading lady in my recovery. Not that it went away easily; rather, it wasn't the main issue to be dealt with. It was simply a manifestation of years — arguably a lifetime — of destructive thinking.

Previously, anxiety was my constant, silent companion, rooted in a kinship with my critical voice. Freedom from it and moments of lightness were what jarred me; peace and feeling calm were strange anomalies and not to be trusted. Now it's the other way around. It now feels strange when I don't feel at peace with myself. My anxiety lets me know, it warns me. Feeling uncomfortable is no longer comfortable. I have a lot to thank my anxiety for, including the journey it's taken me on. To me that is recovery.

The roots of anxiety are in trauma

Close your eyes for a moment and consider what your anxiety really feels like in your body. Are any of these things on your list?

- A sense of impending doom
- Restricted air flow
- Tightness in the chest/throat
- A feeling that you need to respond to something, even if you aren't sure what
- Heart palpitations
- Sweating

- Shaking
- Nausea and gastrointestinal problems

If I asked you what fear feels like, I'd bet the list wouldn't look too different from the one above.

Anxiety is something that plagues so many of us, but my belief is that much of it stems from unprocessed trauma and is actually a state of fear. A thought that leads you down a path of negative self-belief and destruction, a set of physical symptoms – or even a full-blown panic attack.

I lived every day in a constant state of hypervigilance, on high alert for danger at all times – regardless of whether it was logical or understandable to feel threatened – and just thought that I was an anxious and uptight person. Little did I know that I was living with the fallout of unprocessed trauma. When I was living in this state, I often felt frustrated with myself for not being able to function better and for not just getting on with it. It's only with recovery that I've realized I needed to have more compassion towards myself in order to heal these early wounds. Compassion and kindness are so often the keys to resolving or healing conflict, both within ourselves and externally. The more we focus our attention on nurturing a compassionate approach, the more we aid our own healing.

When we start thinking about what we might describe as 'anxiety' and instead give it the label 'fear', we can start to treat it rather differently. Let me explain why that's important . . . Many of the people that I treat in my clinic are victims of trauma. At the root of that trauma is a very scared and fearful child – a child who feels inherently unsafe, unseen and unheard. The ways in which we perceive the world as infants and children become absorbed into our unconscious, and go on to dictate how we view the world as adults.

When we become adults, we walk around thinking that we are anxious and that our anxiety is related to many of the everyday things that we encounter. Yet what we are actually feeling is fear for that past experience. When we think of our symptoms as 'anxiety', we get drawn in to managing those symptoms rather than resolving the original trauma and fostering a sense of safety, which, in turn, stops us feeling fearful.

I myself have experienced how exhausting it is to be hypervigilant, forever in a state of fight or flight with stress hormones pumping around my body. Hypervigilance is something that many abuse survivors live with every single day of their lives, and is very common in those who suffer from trauma. It may be unconscious, and manifest as an overwhelming sense of anxiety rather than a conscious understanding of hypervigilance. Anxiety that has roots residing in trauma isn't (yet) an official diagnosis, but it's certainly associated with anxiety disorders as well as other mental health conditions.

When we start to address our feelings of anxiety as feelings of fear, and when we offer ourselves comfort and self-care in the face of that fear, then the feelings start to disperse. That's because when we are disconnected from our feelings of fear and anxiety, they tend to thrive. But when we notice those feelings, and respond to them with love and kindness, the opposite tends to happen.

Symptoms of fear and anxiety reduce because finally that child within us is feeling seen, heard and taken care of.

Symptoms of anxiety aren't going to disappear overnight, of course, but with time and patience we can learn to cultivate a more loving response to ourselves – and this will help us to heal.

Signs of unprocessed trauma

I believe that unresolved and unprocessed trauma impacts our lives and our choices. A good starting point in exploring this concept can be to see if you identify with any of these indicators of unprocessed trauma . . .

1. You are unable/unwilling to be vulnerable in relationships

Early trauma damages our ability to trust and be vulnerable. So many of us find it nearly impossible to be intimate in relationships, and as a result we struggle to have meaningful connections in both romantic and platonic contexts.

Acknowledging your fear of vulnerability is very much the first step towards healing it. Though it may be true to say that we are terrified of being seen for who we really are, we are also, conversely, desperate for recognition and for our needs to be heard and validated by others. When we begin to notice how often we 'shy away' from showing up as ourselves, we can start to challenge ourselves to engage and connect.

2. You have an internalized sense of inferiority

Left untreated, feelings of inferiority fester and leave us feeling hopeless and useless. Curiosity is a big part of healing. Ask yourself: Why do I feel inferior? What has happened to me that I'm left feeling this way?

We are so ready to accept these self-critical parts of ourselves, and it's only by getting curious as to the origins of these belief systems that we can begin to challenge them. Mindfulness is your friend here, as you begin to observe the patterns of your thoughts and challenge the persistent self-deprecation and unrealistic expectations of how you could or should behave.

3. You believe that you are undeserving of love because you're too fat/ugly/stupid

This feeling is at the core of so many of us who are experiencing unresolved trauma. If you have internalized a belief that you are not deserving of love because you are simply not 'good enough', then you need to consider the possibility that not only might this not be true, but this thought has come from a negative experience you have had that has caused you to accept this view of yourself.

It's only our faith and belief in these thoughts that make them so dangerous. Practising mindfulness allows us to begin to treat them as fleeting thoughts, and they then begin to lose their power.

4. You feel there is something inherently wrong with you

When we do not talk about our trauma or share how we feel, we internalize that pain and it festers. It builds up within us and makes us angry, scared or anxious, and even physically unwell. We have a sense that there is something deeply wrong within us and begin to believe it is *us* that is wrong.

It is the buried trauma and pain that are making us feel this way. When we share our truth with people who are in a position to support us, we can then exorcise that pain. This process can be difficult, but it is what we all need to be able to heal.

5. You are frightened of being 'found out'

We are terrified that if people 'knew' who we really were, we would be rejected. Trauma leaves so many of us feeling incredibly ashamed, and we then do all we can to avoid anyone ever being witness to that shame because it's excruciating. As a result, we then live our lives 'hiding' who we really are, and this reinforces the shameful sense we have of being a fraud or fake in some way.

Even when we try to face this, we often throw ourselves in the deep end and overshare in situations with people who feel unsafe. To truly challenge this belief, we need to create a safe place for ourselves from which to begin to open up carefully and slowly to trusted parties.

6. You feel like a child, unable to cope

When we are exposed to traumatic experiences as children that are not processed or acknowledged, then our emotional growth can become stunted and our sense of self unevolved. In adulthood, our emotional self remains undeveloped, and we are left feeling as though we are children existing in an adult world that we struggle to feel we are able to cope with and process. We don't 'trust' ourselves, and feel persistently overwhelmed and incapable of getting through life.

7. You have a destructive relationship
with food, sex, drugs or alcohol

When we love and care for ourselves, we are not motivated to hurt ourselves. Those of us who develop destructive relationships with food, sex, drugs or alcohol are also struggling to cope with feelings of self-loathing, low self-esteem and an overwhelming sense of not being good enough. These feelings almost exclusively come from the core beliefs that arose in our younger years while struggling to cope with unresolved trauma. But so many of us shrug and accept these feelings as 'normal' and something that we simply have to live with.

The truth is that we don't have to tolerate having such poor relationships with ourselves – and just by considering that we perhaps deserve more, we are challenging the dialogue that we have with ourselves and the world around us. When we consider the roots of these old beliefs, we can begin to heal.

The physical impact of fear and anxiety

Among the most significant aspects of living with persistent fear and anxiety are the various physical symptoms it brings. Nearly all of the clients admitted to my clinic come in with a litany of physical ailments as well as symptoms of mental illness. Many of the people that I work with are suffering from nausea, constipation, cystitis, thrush, indigestion, headaches or general feelings of unwellness. There is also a high proportion of gynaecological issues.

It would be easy to put many of these symptoms down to the fact that sufferers of mental health issues don't always have the most nourishing lifestyle, but I think there's another element to this and our physical and mental selves are inextricably linked. There has been lots of research on the impact of trauma on the body, and you can find this in the suggested reading at the end of the book.

In my experience, when the mind begins to heal, the body begins to follow – and vice versa. In the case of abuse, when a woman feels repelled by her own womanhood because she connects her female form with her trauma, it isn't so surprising that she develops physical symptoms. Gynaecological problems, including chronic pelvic pain, vaginismus and non-specific vaginitis are common diagnoses among abuse survivors. Not only do women who have experienced abuse have a higher rate of these conditions, they may be less likely to have regular sexual health tests or visit the doctor. They may also seek little or no prenatal care.

When we begin to understand the context around our symptoms, we can start on a path towards healing. I have worked with women who have been diagnosed with chronic conditions yet find their symptoms entirely disappear once they have begun to nurture and heal their minds. That's not to say you shouldn't seek medical advice. If you're struggling with numerous physical symptoms then you should certainly consult a doctor, but it's good to also be aware of the link between healing the mind and healing the body.

The 'vicious flower' and changing our thoughts

The vicious flower is a tool that I sometimes use to help people recognize the destructive nature of their thought patterns. Often, simply observing a pattern of thinking that is keeping us trapped allows us to take a step back and change our thinking. The Vicious Flower model (see p. 136) allows us to pinpoint the initial destructive thought, as well as examine how we respond to it and how each thought then perpetuates another.

We can see here that, just by investing in that initial thought, we kick-start a cycle of other destructive thoughts and toxic behaviours that reinforce the initial belief. When I begin working with a client, we'll try to identify some of these destructive patterns and, rather than getting drawn into any attempts at resolution, we simply notice that their anxiety is strong in that moment and trust that the feeling will pass. You might find it helpful to see if you can identify any similar patterns in your own thinking?

Vicious Flower

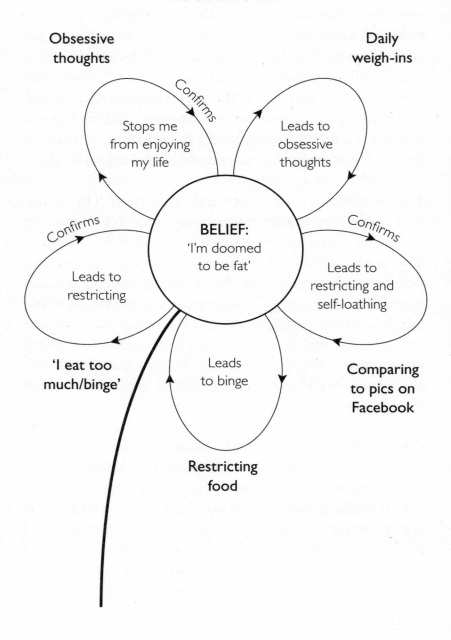

Seeking to eliminate anxiety by resolving every stress and worry that comes along is exhausting. What's more, it doesn't work, because if we really try we can just find something new to worry about. It all comes down to our mood and perspective. After all, when we aren't feeling anxious, we can look at the same situation and not feel so worried. Sometimes we can process a difficult event and self-soothe without getting distressed, and at other times we find ourselves experiencing great anxiety.

So, what lies underneath this anxiety and why does it come along at some times and not others? This is the stuff we need to pay attention to, as it can give us clues as to how we can better take care of ourselves and progress with our recovery.

I'll often ask a client what they would be thinking about if they weren't obsessing over their own inadequacies the whole time. It's always in these moments that I feel the pain in the room rise up, and it becomes obvious that they have been using external distractions as a way of avoiding their own suffering and loneliness. If you feel able, ask yourself a similar question now:

- What would you be thinking about if you weren't thinking about all that you perceive is wrong in your life?
- Is there something that your busy mind could be masking?

#HealHack

Writing down your thoughts in a journal can be helpful when you're starting to create context around what you're experiencing. Giving yourself space to just write and be creative can be an incredible way of accessing parts of yourself that you haven't connected to since childhood. Allow that pen to hit paper, and just see what comes out. Let go of any instinct to control or censor what follows.

Recovery Tool:
Future-Self Journaling

What is future-self journaling?

Future-self journaling is something that I've used for a long time and I'm excited to tell you about it. The version that I love to share was originally developed by a great healer called Dr Nicole LePera, and it is one of the most valuable tools that you can develop to aid your healing and your ability to manifest all that you want into your future. Each day, you give yourself time to follow a set of journaling prompts that are going to help you to manifest, imagine and invest faith in the future self that you are creating.

Simply by giving yourself time to write and visualize a new future for yourself, you are more likely to achieve it. Our realities are formed from our own thoughts – when we take positive action to consciously change our thoughts, then we can manifest a new reality for ourselves.

How do I do it?

Future-self journaling does not require a lot of time but it does require some commitment. You will need to sit for approximately ten minutes each day to focus your attention on the prompts.

We've spoken a lot about the process of healing being one of becoming conscious and making thoughtful and deliberate choices about your future. It takes consistent repetition for this to be truly impactful, so make a commitment to yourself today and make a start.

Step 1: Self-awareness

1. Choose a pattern or a behaviour that you want to change. For example: *I want to prioritize my self-care.*
2. Write affirmations or statements that will encourage and motivate you to achieve this. For example: *I deserve to take care of myself.*
3. Write how you will be able to practise these new behaviours in daily life. For example: *I will make self-care actions of meditation, exercise and journaling the most important tasks of each day.*

After you have completed Step 1, you don't need to complete it again for at least thirty days or until you successfully see change. Then you can introduce a new pattern that you want to challenge.

Step 2: Daily journal prompts

1. Write out your daily affirmation, e.g. *I am worthy of love and respect.*
2. Complete the following journal prompts:

- 'Today I will focus on shifting my pattern to . . .' For example, *Today I will shift my pattern to putting myself first.*
- 'I am grateful for . . .' For example, *I am grateful for my willingness to commit to change. I am grateful for my husband, my dogs, my home.*
- 'The person I am becoming will experience more . . .' For example, *The person I am becoming will experience more joy, abundance and physical peace.*
- 'I have an opportunity to be my future self today when I . . .' For example, *I have an opportunity to be my future self today when I commit to carrying out my self-care exercises.*
- 'When I think about who I am becoming I feel . . .' For example, *When I think about who I am becoming, I feel empowered and hopeful.*

There is no 'right' time to do this work; the most important thing is that you create space where you are able to focus on these questions. I find that early evening works best for me to sit quietly and reflect on my areas for development and growth, but you do what's right for you.

Future-self journaling is something that I've been doing for a very long time, and I've found it massively transformative. It's not only a space to be with myself and hold myself accountable, it's also a wonderful opportunity to reflect on how far I've come and to get inspired.

Step 9: Nurture Your Inner Child

Your inner child needs and wants to be seen,
heard and to feel safe.

Your inner child is the voice within you that represents your child self. Regardless of how old we are, regardless of our status or maturity, we all have an inner child that lives within us and retains all the experiences and beliefs absorbed during our younger years. This chapter is an opportunity to give the wounded child part of yourself a sense of protection, permission and safety.

At this point I should say that I don't think it's 'easy' for many of us to acknowledge what might have been lacking in our childhood. When we begin to explore these early wounds, so many of us feel guilty and as though we are betraying our parents and caregivers. We struggle to admit to the possible absence of nurturing, the neglect, the lack of connection and, in some cases, the abuse. I'm going to remind you now that this is not a process of blame – quite the contrary, this is about owning your truth and validating your own experiences in order to heal.

What is your inner child?

If you were raised in an environment that was challenging to you and in which your emotional and/or physical needs were not met, then your child self will have likely developed a set of beliefs and coping strategies that you may still be using as an adult today. I think, almost without exception, that people feel deeply shamed for having needs that have been ignored by those around them growing up. Often, they report feeling dirty in some way and damaged.

It's vital to recognize that there are basic needs that each of us has and they are totally natural for us as humans. Those feelings of contamination and toxicity around those needs not being met are a result of denying the inner child for so long.

Many of my clients are twisted up with the guilt they feel towards their parents when they begin to acknowledge the pain that they've felt as a result of those relationships. This work that we are doing together is about fostering an understanding and an empathy for all involved. The people who raised us are unconsciously living out their own life scripts, and repeating the same habits and patterns *they* learned in childhood. They, too, are operating from a wounded space because of their own unprocessed emotions.

I often find that this work is an antidote to feeling resentment and anger towards those who parented us, because it allows us to access empathy on a much deeper level. When we recognize that those people that hurt us were also wounded themselves, we can create space to honour our own feelings and to grieve – without being caught up in blaming anyone else.

When our experiences in childhood are not validated by the adults around us, and traumatic experiences are not acknowledged or responded to appropriately, then we become silenced and shamed. When we have to take responsibility for our own physical needs at a young age, like feeding or dressing ourselves, we struggle to nurture ourselves because self-care is just about surviving. When we are raised to take care of younger siblings or a parent, we learn to prioritize others' needs over our own. When we become the confidant of a parent, we lose our childhoods because we are negotiating the complexities of adulthood prematurely. When we are raised by other damaged and wounded people, we struggle to form or maintain intimate relationships of our own.

When things are difficult in a child's world and they're growing up in a dysfunctional environment, that child will often believe either that they are the source of the problem or that they can control themselves and others in order to avoid conflict. Examples of this might include: *If I'm really good then Mummy won't get angry with me.* Or: *If I take care of Daddy when he comes home from work, then he won't get cross with Mummy.*

If you've suffered neglect, trauma or abuse of any kind, you'll have had to shut down this vulnerable child part of yourself and develop a hardened, defensive shell in order to stay safe and to survive. However, that child's pain, grief and anger live on within you, no matter how 'grown-up' you become.

Each of us has our own stories and experiences, and our inner child has stored those memories and their impact upon us. Our inner child is a part of who we are, and it is activated when something triggers us and causes us to feel or react like a child.

Inner child work is so transformative and so healing, but it does take persistence. It can be a strange process to analyse and reframe how you're viewing and responding to a situation, but change is possible. When I did this work, I realized that I wasn't just living with my own set of core beliefs and thoughts, but also inherited ideas that I didn't even have any faith in. I also made a conscious choice to create space for more play, creativity and humour in my life. Repressing my inner child hadn't just silenced opportunities for self-expression, it had also sent the more enchanting childlike qualities of joy and wonder into the shadows as well.

We often connect to the child part of ourselves when our trauma is being triggered, but healing these early wounds will allow you to retain the child within while simultaneously creating space for the compassionate adult self to emerge and respond to difficult and challenging situations.

The critical parent and the compassionate adult

Once we have identified the wants and needs of our inner child, we can begin to consider the tone of our well voice and how it can show up as both a parental figure and a compassionate adult.

The parent voice is something that emerges within us during childhood. It mimics the messages and words of caution that we've absorbed from our primary caregivers, such as: don't play with matches; don't speak to strangers; stop, look and listen when you cross the road.

These are obviously all useful messages that aid our survival and keep us safe. But there are other messages and words of caution that aren't so useful, like: men hurt women and are abusive; certain foods will make you fat; you'll only be happy if you earn lots of money. If our caregivers are unable to recognize that they have maintained an unhealthy belief system, then they will not be able to recognize how destructive it can be to pass certain views on to the children around them.

During recovery, it can be helpful for us to consider our moral and intellectual belief systems, and consider their origins and whether they are helpful or unhelpful to us. We might recognize that maintaining a belief that men hurt women is not only unhelpful but is also something we've unconsciously sought to maintain by seeking out scenarios that sustain that specific belief.

Much of our healing comes when we take a step back and begin to notice how and why we are responding to certain situations (that is, to make the unconscious conscious). When we can identify the voice of the 'parent', we may find that it has merged with the unwell voice. I call this the 'critical parent', and it is yet another manifestation of the unwell voice. It constantly ridicules the inner child, puts them down, ignores their pleas and chastises them.

If we consider how fear is used when guiding a child,

then it's helpful to reflect that fear is a useful tool when it comes to physical safety (e.g. don't play with fire or you'll get burnt) but it can be destructive when it comes to offering emotional guidance. To convey the message that all men hurt women is to offer something entirely subjective and based on one individual's experience rather than literal fact. It is not a rule that will apply to everyone.

Once we've considered the origins of our belief systems and started to reflect on what we want to maintain or challenge, we can start to look for and nurture the 'compassionate adult'. This internal voice is one that comforts, guides and loves. The compassionate adult soothes the inner child and provides tolerance and patience for the journey ahead. When you catch that critical voice emerging, or recognize yourself embracing an old negative belief system, rather than chastising yourself, try giving yourself permission to breathe and consider how you might speak to someone you love in this scenario. Quite often a soothing 'it's okay' or 'I'll get there' is all we need to feel better and continue to move forward.

When you've had a lifetime of negative self-talk, it can take a lot of practice to strengthen this voice – but don't give up, you'll get there. This process can feel pretty clumsy at first and also trigger vulnerability. This doesn't mean that it's wrong. The secret is just to keep going.

Healing the child within

When we first connect with the suffering that our inner child is experiencing, we can feel overwhelmed. Many of us have come to believe (or been led to believe) that the solution to dealing with our past traumas is to repress and ignore them, but actually when we do that we are denying the depth of our experience. We also end up exacerbating our shame.

The irony is that much of the pain that needs to be healed has already been caused by being in an environment where others are also living in a shame-based state. To put it another way: when those raising us struggle to know how to love and care for themselves, they can hardly teach their children to do it.

As we begin to accept the existence of our inner child, we are able to start to heal the hurts of the past. As we acknowledge our inner child, and support and accept all that they have felt, experienced and witnessed, the shame we hold begins to lift. As children, we were powerless to do anything other than survive in the only way that we knew how. We must forgive ourselves for this in order to truly heal at our core.

I spent several months doing some powerful inner child work with a client called Beatrice, who experienced a real shift in acknowledging and embracing her child self:

I had forever associated the childlike me as basically embarrassing and awkward. I felt deep shame when I saw pictures of myself as a child and thought I was 'pathetic' and 'weak'. I had grown up with a mother who had suffered on and off with depression, and I learned pretty early on that her needs would always come before my own. The relationship was confusing, though, and in some ways she was seemingly very available to me, but in other ways, totally absent.

Into adulthood I felt weighed down with sadness and forever felt like I was 'faking it', and I lived in permanent fear of being 'found out' as the bumbling idiot I believed myself to be. Through doing inner child work I was able to connect with a creative part of myself that I simply didn't know. I drew, sketched, moulded, and with messy hands discovered I was able to meet my inner child in previously uncharted territory. When I couldn't find the words, something else took over — and it was there I was able to find comfort.

How to heal

I've discussed the importance of developing a compassionate relationship with yourself. So how do you actually put this into practice? With regards to your inner child, this healing must involve a direct dialogue with this part of yourself and a re-parenting of the self. Your inner child has been ignored and abandoned for so long, and needs plenty of reassurance that you're now here for them and won't abandon them again. This is an opportunity to meet the needs of your child self. In doing so, you repair attachments and will develop more secure and healthy relationships.

Every minute of the day presents an opportunity to be unconditionally compassionate, nurturing and kind to yourself – your inner child needs and wants to be seen, heard and to feel safe. You must be relentlessly kind, promising to listen faithfully to all they have say and to honour their experience without judgement.

In the early years, whenever I heard this voice within myself it just said 'I'm scared' and my response in turn was: *It's okay, I've got this.* I found this whole experience extremely challenging, so if you're finding this a bit woo-woo then believe me, I get it, I really do. But by offering myself this comfort, I found the seeds of self-acceptance, self-belief and a fire inside myself that began to steadily burn as I longed for something more.

This can all take practice, because the unwell voice will often use this sensitive process as an opportunity to criticize and belittle your relationship with your inner child. Your unwell voice will be very invested in minimizing your experiences and denying the true impact that difficult events had upon your life. You need to show up for all the parts of yourself that fear being shamed, betrayed and abandoned. If you can do that, the child part of you will know that they will never be alone again.

Stages of healing

1. **Trust**: In order for your wounded child to begin to find their voice, they must be able to trust that you (the adult) are going to be there. You are going to be the ally who will listen to, validate and comfort your inner child about their early experiences. When you find yourself recalling a

painful memory or feeling a particular trigger, don't ignore or repress it – instead turn towards it and offer yourself a few words of comfort. An acknowledgement of the pain can often go a long way to restoring that trust.

2. **Validation**: It's time to move away from denying, rationalizing, ignoring and minimizing the ways in which you were abandoned, shamed or neglected. This stage is one of accepting your truth and acknowledging that these experiences wounded you on some deep level.

3. **Grief**: Coming to terms with our truth and validating our own experiences can be painful. We can feel sadness, shock and anger – all of these emotions are a natural part of grieving. Facing these truths gives us an opportunity to shift and challenge dysfunctional family systems, and create new patterns of enlightened awareness.

4. **Loneliness**: Coming to terms with the wounds that were created in childhood can leave us feeling shameful and lonely. Our inner child feels flawed and damaged somehow. They have learned to hide this part of themselves, but as adults we live with imposter syndrome and a fear of being found out. By loving ourselves and showing ourselves unrelenting kindness and compassion, we coax the secret parts of ourselves out of hiding. We learn to connect and respect all of ourselves.

5. **Identify current manifestations:** Doing this work will shine a light on how early wounds are manifesting in destructive and damaged behaviours today. Becoming aware and conscious of these connections is a huge part of making a shift towards healthier and more compassionate behaviours.

6. **Fill in the gaps:** When we begin to identify the traumas and wounds that we experienced in childhood and how they are impacting us as adults, we have an opportunity to meet those needs in the here and now. For example, if as a child we were used to being let down, then we can make a commitment to our inner child to make and keep small promises to ourselves, and so gain their confidence and trust. If we felt as though our needs were ignored or neglected as a child, then we can make a commitment to seek and nurture relationships where we are able to voice and meet our needs. As painful as looking back can be, it's sometimes the only way of moving forward.

At this stage, I often remind my clients that grieving is one of the most natural and healing processes in the world. We move through stages (shock, anger, sadness, acceptance) in order to allow us to manage the events of our lives. If this process becomes repressed or halted, then so too does our healing.

In order to heal our inner child, we must allow our true

feelings to emerge. We must accept those feelings without judgement and offer ourselves compassion, time and the space to grieve, until we arrive at a place where we fully accept who we are.

We are all yearning for connection with others, but we must remember that we had it once. In childhood we perceived the world with awe; we had value, and we viewed ourselves with joy and wonder. We were whole, we were connected, we were present. Then experiences and outside influences happened and this internal peace was corrupted.

#HealHack

If you are struggling to allow yourself compassion, see if you can find a photograph of yourself as a baby or as a small child. Spend some time looking at that photograph, and try not to make any judgements. Just work on making a connection with yourself as you were then.

Recovery Tool:
Mood Shifters

It can be so hard to find the strength to keep going when that unwell voice inside you is talking really loudly. That's why I've created this list of potential 'mood shifters' – six easy things you can do to help get your positive mojo going again. Obviously, you can add your own to this list – the more mood shifters you have in your toolbox, the better!

A personal check-in

When I'm working with people, they initially may find it challenging to connect to how they are feeling and to the experience of being alive. Reigniting a connection between body and soul is part of the healing process. Yet when we're busy interacting with others or rushing through our day, we can forget to 'check in' with ourselves to see where we're at and what we need. Try to get into the habit of stopping occasionally, taking a breath and tuning in with yourself, both mentally and physically.

What if you don't know how you're feeling? Just start with the basics – your body will often give you clues as to what you are feeling mentally or what you may need physically, and it's just about learning to decipher those. For example, if your shoulders are hunched and tight, this could mean that you are feeling stressed or tense. If your jaw is locked, you might be angry; if your stomach is churning, you could be fearful; and if your legs are aching, then perhaps you simply need a rest! These are just suggestions; there aren't any hard and fast rules about what any physical sensation might be representing because everyone is different.

Try to get curious about your body and learn what it's trying to tell you, because, over time, making small changes in response to your body's signals can have a profoundly positive effect on your wellbeing. Don't worry if this process takes a while to get good at – like learning any new skill, it requires patience and perseverance.

An act of random kindness

Often we focus our attention on what we're getting, without considering what we're investing. But so much of my own healing has come from supporting others in need. If you're finding yourself in a mental funk, then try practising an act of kindness towards someone else.

Kindness is possibly my favourite human quality, because it's so rewarding and literally makes the world a nicer place to be. I find kindness so inspiring and powerful, and I love observing it in others. My husband, Thom, is so casually kind to anyone that crosses his path, whether that's him smiling at a stranger, making a cup of tea for someone living on the street or offering up his time to someone who might need his help. Kindness is contagious, and the more your practise it, the better you'll feel.

Go for a walk in silence

I'm very mindful that, when I go out walking, I don't always stick my headphones in my ears to fill my head with noise. I'm not saying I don't love music, podcasts or audiobooks, or even calling friends, but there's something very rewarding about giving yourself time to just be alone and in silence. I've noticed that when I'm wandering about in silence I take in more of my surroundings – the colour of the sky, the wildlife, what the air feels like and smells like on that day. I also love the inspiration that appears when I don't fill my head with information. I go out with the intention of being present in nature, but come home with fresh ideas and a clearer, calmer mind.

Getting organized

I learned really early on in life that if I want my mind to feel calm, then my environment must 'feel' calm as well. It's very difficult to feel at peace with yourself when you're surrounded by chaos.

De-cluttering your space, organizing your clothes, cleaning the kitchen or doing other 'life admin' can help you to feel more peaceful internally. It's also a really great way of positively distracting yourself from negative thoughts. Just a few simple tasks like clearing out a desk or sorting out your miscellaneous paperwork can help stop you ruminating on worries and shift some energy around for the better.

Watch the right stuff

One of the rules I live by is never to watch the evening news. I think it's really destructive to fill my mind with images and talk of war, loss and pain just before I'm about to go to bed (and unfortunately this is pretty much the sole content of the news today). Instead I choose to keep myself updated with what's going on in the world by reading certain publications and chatting to people whose views I value.

I'd recommend that if you decide to watch something in the evening, you consider your mood and what you might need most by way of entertainment. For example, if you know that you're feeling down or vulnerable, then watching something that makes you laugh can really help. My personal visual healing generally comes in the form of films starring Bill Murray and anything written by Julia Davies! It might sound trite but, honestly, if you're trying to shift from living a life that's dictated by an unwell voice, then a little laughter goes a long way.

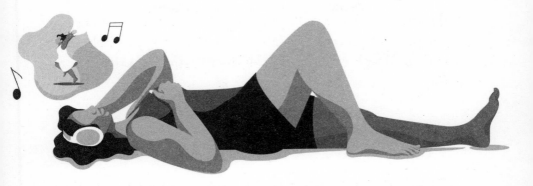

Listen to music

Music is a wonderful way of connecting with emotions, especially when we're struggling to find words to articulate what's going on for us. Music also has the power to create massive internal shifts in how we're feeling, and – provided we pick music that lifts rather than lowers our mood – it can be very helpful in pulling us out of a downward spiral and changing our mental state.

Seek out artists that connect to your soul and inspire you; ask friends what they are listening to; and go and see live music whenever you have the opportunity. Creating space where you give yourself time to really *listen* to music can be incredibly healing, so think about that the next time you reach for your TV's remote control.

Step 10: Manifest Your Future

Recovery is about more than just an absence of symptoms.

This is where life gets really exciting. This is the point at which we are able to visualize the future that we want, and are growing in confidence that we have the tools we need to achieve it. I think sometimes we can feel a little overwhelmed at this point – I certainly remember realizing how much power I had to create my own future, and as thrilling as that idea was, it was also pretty scary! I'd spent so long feeling helpless and being in a victim state that it took me some time to really own my power. If you're feeling in a similar way, then I get it – and trust me, you just need to keep putting one foot in front of the other, and you're going to get to where you need to go.

Building self-confidence and feeling good now

Now that you're starting to truly understand how your unwell voice operates, and are a little wiser to it, we can start to focus on the future. It's time to take your first steps in the world as a happier, more self-aware and reflective person.

This part of the journey isn't like early recovery – which can often feel like a hard, exhausting slog – though in many ways it is just as important. Why? Because it's about living the life you truly want, instead of the one you perhaps thought you deserved. We are now going to focus on building on the foundations of nurturing your relationship with yourself – a relationship that I believe is worthy of lots of love and attention.

There are so many people in the world who simply don't believe that things can change – they don't think that how they view themselves and the world can ever be any different. What's remarkable, however, is that you've already made changes – and those changes came directly from self-belief. Taking those first steps is really, really hard, so I hope you're truly proud of yourself. I'm confident that you're going to look back at this chapter of your life and feel inspired by all you've achieved.

What often happens in recovery is that people get drawn into focusing *only* on their harmful and painful symptoms. Then, once they've stabilized some of their destructive behaviours, they stop their journey there, as if *not* engaging in unhealthy behaviours is the very best that they could hope for. In my clinic, however, we think that's not the whole story. After all, you probably know by now that the changes you needed to make in order to get to this stage came from the inside, beneath the skin. They weren't entirely about those damaging behaviours – those were more a representation of how you felt about yourself at your core.

I believe recovery offers an opportunity to go much

further than just healing old wounds and learning to take care of yourself (though those two things are massive, of course). To make a full recovery we need to forge a relationship with our entire selves that is both strong and compassionate, and is also based on a decent level of self-esteem. It's about embracing a whole new way of living – and, what's more, the journey of self-development is never-ending. There's always room to grow and to be inspired by something new. For me, there are always relationships that I want to develop and nurture, especially the relationship that I have with myself.

Let me say this clearly: you are capable of great things. Much of what you believed you were capable of in the past was a product of a limiting belief system that you developed during childhood. First of all, any limiting belief systems restrict our potential; and second, they stop us accessing both joy and peace. Don't worry, though – if you're committed to yourself and dedicated to your recovery, you'll be guided towards what you really need in order to continue healing.

Don't lament the past

I've heard so many people lamenting the past, regretting choices they made and wishing that they'd found recovery sooner. My response to that is this: of all the painful and traumatic experiences that I've been through, none have been pointless. Much as I would never wish to relive these experiences, I am able to recognize the valuable lessons in each of them and therefore I don't wish them away.

I've learned some of the most vital lessons in life with pain as my teacher. When feeling alone and hurting I've turned to visionaries like Glennon Doyle, Brené Brown, John Bradshaw and India Arie. I learned that my pain was a resource for me, and that by reflecting and challenging myself to be and want more, I had an opportunity to change my life.

You are on a journey, and throughout this journey there's no doubt that you'll meet challenges. If you can trust that you have the tools to face whatever comes your way, then each challenge is an opportunity to learn and to grow. What's more, if you find yourself veering off course or hitting a bump in the road, you can just take a little step back, reflect on your experience and then keep moving forwards.

You can do this.

Your thoughts create your world

Manifestation is the process of actively bringing the things we desire into our lives. It is a simple process, but it takes practice to shift your mindset to recognizing that you are powerful and that you have the capacity to create your own reality.

When we think positively and have a strong sense of self-belief, our external world reflects that. When our thoughts are full of happiness, hope, prosperity, abundance and joy, it is all those things that manifest in our world. We attract better opportunities, more loving people and a life that is in line with all of our hopes and dreams.

On the other hand, when we've been living with an unwell voice inside our head for a long while and are immersed in negative thinking, then our worlds will reflect our sadness and the toxic nature of that internal voice. We miss out on opportunities, we attract negative relationships and we become sicker, both physically and mentally.

It's important to note that if you're still struggling with your unwell voice, then it's likely that it has *plenty* to say about my ideas here! I'm fairly sure too that any commentary it offers will be based on fear, rather than faith. Please remind yourself not to trust that unwell, critical voice. Having faith that you (and everyone around you) can achieve what you (and they) dream of, and then manifesting that, is something that I can tell you from my own experience really does work. I created this career that I have; I manifested the relationship that I'm in; I wished my children into my life. I am thankful every single day, because I know what the alternative was. And I've not only witnessed this power in my own life, but also in the lives of my clients. I've seen it numerous times in fact: once people remove the obstacles in their lives (self-doubt, fear, procrastination) and replace that with self-belief and faith, they really are able to achieve all that they've been wanting.

Another wonderful client, Chrissy, described how achieving a sense of self-love became the focus of her recovery:

My commitment to manifesting all that I wanted is the vow that I made to myself. I promised to myself that though I'd lost myself once, I would fight to stay holding onto myself forever. And one day it was no longer a fight. I got the chance to see myself as the beautiful, vibrant, talented and loving woman that I am, the woman who just wants to help heal the world as she once healed herself. I feel grateful for the woman I am and even more grateful to know that no matter what happens, self-love will always be my number-one rule! I made it, and now I'm living a life I couldn't have even fathomed.

I should probably add a small caveat – this doesn't mean that we will never be faced with difficulty again. What faith means for me is merely that when I'm confronted with something testing, I can ask myself, *What can I learn from this – what can I take from it to help me grow and develop, to become a better version of who I am right now?*

When I look back on my past experiences and the difficult things I've had to face, I can see that each of those challenges brought me to a stronger place – a place where I feel really good about who I am and better able to support others. In other words, my life experiences have given me the knowledge, insight and tools to allow me to create the life that I want to live and also have a bigger impact on the world.

If you're in the habit of thinking in an especially self-defeating way, it's worth taking some time to consciously start noticing what, exactly, you're thinking about from hour to hour. If this sounds tricky, go first towards how you are feeling – it's usually a good marker for what's going on inside our mind, because when we're feeling anxious, stressed or uptight, then we're probably thinking critical or fearful thoughts.

This process isn't about controlling feelings, but rather about observing thoughts. When we realize that we are ruminating on unhelpful thoughts, we have the choice to shift our focus to something else, thus changing the thoughts. This will weaken the unwell voice, which needs all our attention in order to stay strong. This is why when we start thinking about forging a beautiful future as a well and happy person, the power of the illness automatically begins to diminish.

Manifesting what we want

It's common at this point in recovery to become a bit dissatisfied. Lots of people complain to me that they've been setting an intention about what they want to do, have or achieve, but they don't feel that the universe is delivering!

One of the things I've learned is that, when I've been fixated on a specific outcome or product, I've become drawn into believing that I know what is right for me – or I've tried to rigidly control the route my life should take. From experience, I can tell you now that this isn't actually helpful. The secret to manifesting what you want is to let go of how things might happen – the exact way you think things should materialize – and instead simply invest your faith in the belief that what is meant for you is on its way.

Once you can do this, you'll be amazed: it's such a relief to let go of the burden of having to plan out every detail of how your future is going to look! Now you can really let go, knowing that the universe already has things figured out and your job is simply to have faith, take inspired action and enjoy the ride while trusting that whatever form your future takes, it's exactly as it's meant to be.

Acknowledging fear and doubt

At this point I think that it's important to acknowledge how challenging this transition to letting go can be. Many of us are raised with a clear picture of what life *should* look like, and the sequence of events that we *expect* ought to take place.

Let me give you an example from my own experience. Back when I was committed to a path of duty and expectation, my fear of drifting from the supposed plan prevented me from connecting with many potentially wondrous experiences. I was raised to follow a very specific route of working hard and studying hard (in order to go university) so that I could get a job, get married and have children. Essentially, what I learned as a child was that I should marry someone wealthy because there was no money in any kind of creative career. I was raised to believe that this was the only way for me to find success and happiness.

Many of us don't flourish under these kinds of constraints, though, do we? I didn't end up realizing my potential by trying to go down the more academic path I'd been taught to follow. I began to understand that what

I was expecting for myself – the person I was expecting myself to be – actually just made me miserable, so I turned my focus towards a more appreciative way of thinking, embracing a more creative path and trusting in beauty. This gave me a sense of the divine and allowed me to consider that there was something greater than myself out there, and I started to break away from the restrictive life I had been living and move towards a more intuitive, freer way of being.

Here are the questions I asked myself, and which I'd now like you to ask yourself: *Am I living my life like it's a story – one that's already written and printed out? And if I am, then is that story empowering me or hurting me?*

When I reflected on this myself, I changed the way I did things. I became entirely motivated by what inspired me in life, instead of what I thought I *should* be doing. I started to consider what made me feel alive – all the things that really flooded my soul and mind with joy and excitement.

What makes me happy? I asked myself. *What do I adore? What change would I like to see in the world? What can my contribution be?*

Now ask yourself those questions too.

Abandonment of the self (true loneliness)

We are trained by society to focus on obtaining material things to gain personal satisfaction. Yet there's no real success without deep personal fulfilment, is there?

I've gained the deepest sense of peace and fulfilment through nurturing key relationships in my life, and by working to make a difference around the issues that I see impacting all of us.

Living a life that is totally controlled by fear and an all-encompassing sense of loathing is a total abandonment of the self – hence why it's such an isolating state to be in. The unwell voice makes us betray all of our physical and emotional needs, denying us things like food, sleep and self-care. It tells us we don't need to have a voice in the world, and forces us to compromise on who we are.

Time to create your future

In essence, manifestation is an energy that allows us to summon something tangible into our lives through attraction and belief. When you begin to understand the power of manifestation and witness your ability to shape your own future, this new way of living will simply become a new way of being

1. Be clear about what you want

When I begin to explore what people want, I find that they get very focused on looking backwards and naming what they *don't* want. When you have spent a lifetime ignoring your own wants and needs, it can be challenging to connect to who you really are and what you actually want from life. Try to embrace this process, and allow yourself some time to explore, reflect and figure out what it is you're interested in, what you need and what you want.

Remember to keep your wellbeing at the centre of everything that you want, and be mindful of not limiting your desires to what you previously believed is possible. You can have whatever you want. You just need to be clear about what that is.

2. Have faith

This process is not about daydreaming; it is about actively creating your future. You have the ability to manifest your hopes and dreams into your life by believing that they are possible. It is important that once you have identified what you want, you *ask for it* and believe that it will be delivered to you at the right time. Imagine for a moment that you already have what you desire. How would you act? How would you talk? How would you walk, think, feel, dress and make decisions? Your job is to ask for what you want and then to let go and have faith that what you want is on its way – and to live, feel and act as if it's already been delivered, until it becomes your natural state of being.

3. Visualize your future self

When we can see ourselves doing something, it becomes a lot easier to have faith in that possibility. Our brains do not know the difference between our physical reality and a thought. When we can see ourselves living the life that we want to live, our minds respond and we feel happier, more peaceful and more content. Spend five minutes a day visualizing yourself living your dream life, in as much detail as possible. Where are you? Who are you with? What are you doing? What can you see, smell, hear, taste and touch? Focus on the sensations and feelings, and do what you can to make them as real as possible.

If you're finding visualizing challenging, then try writing a description of what you and your life are like in six months. Focus on the changes that you have made in your life and how they have positively impacted you. Allow yourself to sink into the emotion of the reality you are creating. Keep doing this over and over, to strengthen your feelings around it. If you find that unwell voice creeping in and using this as an opportunity to make you feel inadequate about where you are today, just breathe and trust that where you are right now is exactly where you are meant to be. This is a process of moving forward.

4. Take inspired action

When we are clear about what we want and we have faith in manifesting our future, the way to achieve it will become clear to us. This is where letting go is so valuable. When we try to control our experiences too much, we can become blind to opportunity and our rightful path. When we trust that the next steps will be revealed to us at the right time, we can relax and enjoy the process. The 'how' will be shown to us.

In the early days of my own healing journey, I spent a lot of time worrying and controlling how things were going to work, but as soon as I let go and trusted in the process

I realized that I was able to relax, knowing that the universe had a plan for me and that my job was to simply ask, believe and trust. You can do this too: give yourself time to cultivate a new way of thinking and being, and you will get there.

5. Daily self-care

We all resist what is unfamiliar to us, and it's perfectly normal to have doubts about something new. Faith exists on faith alone, so don't wait for evidence to be delivered to you before you are willing to invest. Take a leap.

Make a decision to change your life, invest in daily self-care rituals and prioritize your wellbeing. So many of us have our self-care behaviours at the bottom of a long list that we may or may not get around to. But when our self-care is our number-one priority, then everything else gets easier. Nurture your body through movement, support your mind through meditation, and offer yourself daily mantras that keep you on track: *Today I behold all of the abundance that surrounds me.*

Smile now, knowing that everything is going to change; feel the emotion of being fulfilled and at peace. Practise this daily.

6. Show up

So much of this journey is about waking up and showing up in our own lives. We are already manifesting our realities, and by remaining present and mindful you choose to do so consciously, creatively and with positive intention.

Pay close attention to the ways that the universe begins to communicate to you that things are beginning to shift.

Be open to meeting new people, hearing new ideas and embracing new opportunities. Enjoy the excitement that you are going to feel in knowing that what you want is on its way.

7. Practise gratitude

When life is difficult and we've become caught in a negative cycle of just surviving, we experience very little. We live our lives as victims of our experiences, as opposed to conscious creators. As you begin this new chapter of your life, focus your intention on gratitude for what you already have in your life that you are thankful for. Feeling grateful shifts our energy onto a frequency of abundance, and allows us to attract more of what we want into our lives. Writing lists of all you have to be grateful for will instantly help you to feel more positive and connected *right now*.

At this point I'd like to share Christina's story. Christina's persistence was key to achieving all that she wanted. I think she encapsulates so much of what many of us have felt or gone through at different times, and how sometimes there is joy in just feeling authentic.

Recovery for me has been a journey to a destination I never knew existed. I spent my life from a young age accepting that I had to change myself, believing I was not enough and that I was inadequate as a person. To me, this transformation to a place of inner acceptance is truly remarkable.

I don't even think I believed such a place of self-acceptance existed (well, not for me). I certainly never thought I could be a woman who cultivated a relationship with myself of self-care and self-respect. It seemed incomprehensible that I would ever not be reliant on over-the-counter or prescription medications to a) be happy or b) lose weight.

I now embrace all areas of myself; I don't compartmentalize, split myself or hide pieces of who I am to try and fit to those around me in a desperate bid to be accepted. For me, the weight of shame was a heavy burden and fed my destructive behaviours on a massive scale. I had shame in what felt like all areas of my life: shame around my weight and appearance; shame of my sexuality; and shame of failed relationships and failures in my career.

I've come to learn that every life experience (including the dark and painful ones) is important, and they have made me who I am — and I am a stronger and more confident person for it. Most importantly, I don't hide those parts of myself any more.

Healing has not been linear; it has felt messy and I have been deeply conflicted at points, as it felt as if I was betraying my ambitions to be perfect by going to therapy and that I was being unfaithful to that old friend . . . the unwell voice.

I honestly thought I was in control of my destructive behaviours and that I had the power to stop. I believed that I had boundaries that I wouldn't cross and didn't view myself as 'unwell'. The reality was that, in the end, I had crossed every single boundary I had; I ate food out of the bin, vomited in public places and took more laxatives and slimming pills than I ever thought possible. I became more obsessive and judgemental of others, and abandoned every moral value that I had. I was convinced that if I lost enough weight and looked a specific way, I would finally be enough. Be lovable. Be popular. Be accepted. I strived for perfection in every area of my life; in the end all this meant was that I was setting myself up to fail by setting my standards so high no one could reach them — not even me.

I am still devastated by the friendships I lost, the years of my life gone to self-loathing. The unwell voice made it impossible for anyone to get close. I was fiercely protective of my behaviours and I behaved in a selfish and self-obsessed way, all to try to protect my secret. Because while I believed my tools for control would be my salvation, I was also deeply ashamed of them.

I remember so many times being sat with my GP or Community Mental Health Team worker and being told I didn't meet the threshold to receive treatment. All this did was further confirm my beliefs that it was actually fine to be this unhappy in yourself, and that it was normal to be consumed by fear. I had found myself in a space where I had no idea who I was any more.

I can honestly say that, for me, talking is the single biggest tool in my recovery kit. By talking to someone — whether that was friends, family or colleagues — about my struggles, I directly challenged the shame and stigma I was carrying about my bulimia and my sexuality. However, I'm acutely aware of how difficult and painful it can be to talk to even your closest friends. I can say without hesitation that I wouldn't be in recovery if it wasn't for all the amazing people who have sat with me, talked to me, listened to me and at times sat by my side in silence, sometimes for hours.

The more I talked and opened up, the more things started to shift. It was indeed slow, but every time I shared my secrets and things I felt ashamed of, it shone light into dark pieces of my soul that had never been seen or heard before. I had thought that the unwell voice was unique to me; little did I know that for years I would sit in a circle with other women who also lived with the same shackles around their lives, crippling them. I would hear them recount almost word for word anecdotes of my life and my experiences. Because of this I now know that I was never really alone.

For years I lived my life as a person who always felt alone — I guess I was trying to find somewhere to belong, somewhere I didn't have to hide myself. Now I am me, all of me, a nurse and a nanny, a lesbian and a Christian, who is also a recovered bulimic, who has a love of being organized and a passion for cocktails and dancing.

I never thought a joyful life was possible for me; but it's given me the opportunity to change my career, go backpacking solo and come out as a lesbian! But above all of that, I now know who I am and I don't hate myself. Not every day is perfect — this process of growth is in many ways ongoing through life, facing new opportunities and challenges, but I know that I have the strength to make it through because I've been through hell and back and I'm still standing to share the story.

Be compassionate and patient with yourself. Every time you feel yourself engaging in old negative patterns of behaviour, lovingly steer yourself back on course. Your quest ultimately is to pursue a more joyful state, so seek out people and experiences that keep your emotional state high. Go and embrace your life — your time is now.

#HealHack

Slow down. So often we spend most of our days running from one appointment to another, without giving ourselves space to think. Slowing down allows us to begin to reflect on how compassionate we are being towards ourselves, and gives us time to think about whether the choices we are making are in our best interests.

Recovery Tool: Letters to and from Your Inner Child

Why send messages to and from your inner child?

It's time to focus on manifesting a life full of meaning and purpose, and to be guided by something that instinctively feels right – intuition or your well voice.

Your willingness to nurture your inner child and listen to your well voice will allow you to look into the future and see yourself as wiser, more grateful and happier than ever before. Developing and maintaining a positive connection and ongoing relationship with the inner child has been a huge part of my own recovery. It's a really important aspect of healing our traumas – we need to learn to understand this wounded part of ourselves and to offer it kindness because, even as an adult and after years of treatment and healing, we can still find ourselves triggered and hurtled back emotionally to a time when we were hurt as a child.

So many of us felt unseen, unheard or misunderstood as young people. Writing to – and connecting with – our inner child can help us to heal these wounds. Try thinking about what you might like to say to your five-year-old self, for example, if you were given the chance. What about your eleven-year-old self, or your sixteen-year-old self? Each of us has an inner child within us, yet as life goes on we often block them out or build walls around them to help us cope with difficult past experiences or memories.

Of course, that inner child shows up in varying ages – and, since we change a great deal throughout our younger years, I like to suggest that my clients create a series of letters, each of which is written to their younger self at a different life stage. I suggest writing these letters to yourself at these following stages: baby self, toddler self, primary school self and then one letter between eleven and eighteen (four letters in total). Each of those versions of you will have had different needs, hopes and desires, and it's important we honour them all.

This can be a deeply healing and poignant experience. It can, at times, also be intense and even unsettling. If you don't feel in a strong enough position to take on this task, then please wait until you feel ready or take advice from a clinician.

Writing a letter from your inner child to your adult self

Find a quiet place when you have the time and space to feel safe and able to be vulnerable. If possible, get a photograph of yourself at the age of the self you're writing to, and spend a few minutes looking at it. If you don't have a photograph, conjure up a memory instead. Really try to close yourself off to your world as it is now, and simply imagine being with yourself as you were in the photograph or memory.

Next, consider what your child self wants to say to you as an adult. What do they want you to know or to hear at this point in your life?

Once you have a sense of what your inner child would like to communicate, you can begin to write your letter. Be mindful once again of all the emotions that are coming up for you, and be sure to be gentle and kind to yourself.

An example of a letter:

Dear [adult you],

I feel lost and scared and I need your help. My parents are fighting and angry and I'm frightened something bad will happen. I don't know what to do.

Please listen to me and don't leave me alone any more.

Love [child you].

Writing a letter to your inner
child from your adult self

Begin as you did with your previous letter, by finding a quiet place where you have enough time and space to allow yourself to be vulnerable. Connect with whatever image you've got of yourself at the age that you're focusing on, and spend time really inhabiting that part of you.

Now, consider what you might like to say to this version of yourself, or what you might offer. What did you need to hear at this stage that you perhaps were never told? If you had the chance, what would you say?

After taking some time to think about this, you can begin to write your letter. Keep in mind the age of the self that you're writing to: a letter to a baby will likely be far shorter than a letter to a young teen.

This can get emotional. Try to breathe through it and really feel everything that comes up for you, though. If you find yourself overwhelmed at any point, then give yourself permission to take a break for as long as you need. Come back to the letter whenever you're ready.

Example of a letter:

Dear [child you],

I am here to love, protect and care for you. I will honour the things that you lack and I will accept you for all you are today. I want you to know that it is safe for you to express all of your needs, and for you to be seen and heard. I will create space for you to express your creativity and for you to explore your talents and gifts.

I will be here for you whenever you need me. I love you so much.

Love [adult you].

Once you have written your letters, take some time to process what has been communicated. This process of connecting with your inner child is a powerful one – only you can heal the pain for this part of yourself; and love, compassion and kindness are the antidotes to any deep wounds.

Step 11: Discover Your Spiritual Self

There is nobody else in the world like you,
and celebrating that is a beautiful thing.

Over the years I've spoken to a lot of different clinicians, healers, therapists and people in recovery about what they think is ultimately the most important thing about healing and developing a compassionate relationship with themselves. Without exception they all say the same thing: to develop some sort of spiritual connection with yourself and something greater than yourself. I've gone on a great journey with this myself – beginning as the darkest sceptic and ending with a connected and grounded sense of *who I am*, which exists beyond *what I am*.

I've included this as the last chapter because I think it's the final part of what really makes us whole. If you've worked through the book implementing all the recovery tools, then you might well have already started to ask yourself some of the bigger 'why' questions. Lean in to that curiosity; culturally we're not necessarily encouraged to explore this part of ourselves, but for me it's been really transformational.

What is spirituality?

Spirituality is an important element of living a peaceful and contented existence – it is something that needs nurturing, and can be a particularly powerful resource for those recovering from mental illness. At the clinic, our Spiritual Group is a warm and safe space where members can begin to explore their relationship with their own spirituality.

When I ask clients how they imagine the spiritually minded to be, they often paint a picture of people who are totally unfazed by life's daily stresses and dramas, floating around on little Zen clouds. They find it difficult to imagine a version of spirituality that works for them.

But spirituality isn't something evasive – and whoever you are, it's not out of reach. It needn't be an aspect of life that's reserved for the overtly religious, or for people on pilgrimages to faraway lands. In fact, it can be a whole lot more accessible and relatable than that.

In my view, spirituality doesn't have to include any particular religious faith or denomination, and it can be totally free of organized or institutionalized structures. For me, at its simplest it is the deep and intimate relationship that any individual develops with something bigger than themselves. It involves the recognition that there's something more to being human than what can be materially seen or felt, and invites a belief that there is something divine existing within nature and the universe. Spirituality is learning to tap in to a greater source of grace, peace and love within you.

Through developing a spiritual practice, we are able to nurture a conscious and mindful appreciation of life and the universe at large. We are able to see and accept that there isn't always a rational or scientific explanation for things, and we instead develop a sense of faith that's built upon something else entirely.

Regardless of where your starting point is – whether you already have a strong sense of something beyond yourself, or have actively dismissed that notion up until now – you can still cultivate and nurture a relationship with your spiritual self from this point forward.

There's another point about all this that I want to make

here, and it relates to you and you alone. There is nobody else in the world like you, and celebrating that (and the unique gifts you have to offer) is a beautiful thing. Yes, you matter to those who love you, but it's more than that too. You and your contribution also matter to the world at large. You are a miracle, part of a universal love, and appreciating this will help to move and inspire you, in turn influencing how you think and feel. When people connect to this spirituality, this all-encompassing loving, compassionate and kind energy – as opposed to connecting to mistrust, pain and fear – they are able to align with a sense of purpose within the world.

So how do we describe or envisage our spirituality? Some of my clients refer to it as a 'faith in the universe', while others call it a 'guardian angel' or a 'power greater than myself'. But really, the terms we use to describe it are far less important than developing it. One of the most key things about cultivating a spiritual life is that, in our most desperate and painful moments, it's this spiritual connection that helps us through – by reminding us that our experiences are part of something greater, of a shared human experience, and that, as a result, we're not alone.

Spirituality is important in healing a damaged relationship with ourselves, because the unwell voice relies so much on us living in metaphorical darkness – the kind of darkness in which self-loathing and fear can thrive. Fear is our mind's immediate response to the unfamiliar, and while there's nothing wrong with that, the key is not getting stuck in fear-based thought patterns and behaviours. Once we begin to connect and explore our relationship with our spirituality, however, we welcome in the light and the unwell voice can no longer survive.

As such, I believe that stress and pain are a communication from our heart that we are not tending to our spiritual needs. Continue to recognize when you are thinking thoughts of fear, and replace them with thoughts of love; carry on working that compassionate well voice and strengthening it. In theory, the idea of replacing unwell thoughts with thoughts of self-love is pretty simple; what's challenging is overcoming the obstacles your unwell voice presents and your resistance to doing something different. By embracing a new practice, and shifting your focus in order to tend more to your spiritual self, you'll see and feel a positive shift in your energy.

How to develop a spiritual practice

For many of us, the unfamiliar task of developing a spiritual practice can seem daunting. That's because your practice involves the wonderful (albeit courageous) task of removing the blocks that exist between you and your spiritual self.

One of the critical blocks that might cause a problem, for example, is your unwell voice telling you you're not deserving of love. This (as I've said before) is *not* to be trusted and is quite simply untrue: love is a part of your spiritual being, and it already resides within you.

Here are some tips for developing your spiritual practice . . .

Nurture your faith in your universe

Spirituality is about having faith and trusting in your life path. It's not up to you to try to control or manipulate your journey – only to believe that you are where you are meant to be at any given time.

When I speak about this in a recovery group, I often get people saying, 'Yes, but how can I accept I have a mental illness and also trust that this is where I am meant to be?' My response is usually the same: although suffering with a mental illness is painful and difficult, it's also what has brought them there, to a place where they're exploring their relationship with themselves and others and reflecting on their spirituality. That in itself is incredibly valuable.

Surrendering to your life is a big part of recovery – to know that you cannot control everything, and to trust that there *is* a plan for you. In the earliest stages of recovery, that process of surrender needs to be a conscious and mindful process, but ultimately what we're aiming for is a way of living where you no longer need to sweat the small stuff because you can trust that things will unfold just as the universe intended. No more obsessing about what you think you should have or shouldn't have, or how you think your future should or shouldn't look. Instead, simply focus your intention on receiving all of the love and wonder that the universe has to offer.

Trust that you have a purpose

A lack of purpose in life is often a significant factor in the development of anxiety, depression and phobias.

When we are able to cultivate trust and faith in the face of the unknown, and to accept uncertainty as an uncontrollable part of life, we are able to really let go – and it's amazing.

Your life reflects the thoughts that you have about yourself. Developing your spiritual self allows you to view yourself as empowered and in a state of healing, and you can choose to give meaning to that too. It took a long time for me to have a clear sense of my own purpose, which I believe is about connecting to my own spiritual journey – as well as encouraging and supporting others to recognize their potential via this same spiritual connection. Even now, however, I recognize that there's more to come; and I may not be aware of future work I have to do or the roles I'll need to play. But throughout this uncertainty, I can trust the universe to show me these things whenever the time is right.

Forgive yourself

Several years ago I went to see an inspirational speaker talking about cultivating a spiritual practice. First, she offered her guidance, and then she opened the session up to questions from the floor. One brave middle-aged man raised his hand in a room full of a thousand people (predominantly women) and spoke about his shame concerning how he had behaved in the past. He shared how he had objectified women and cheated on his wife. He talked about how his marriage had broken down as a result of his behaviour, and how he was now restricted from spending time with his young daughter – though it was she who had provided him with much of his motivation to change. He wept openly and said that, although he recognized that he was now living a different life, he was unable to forgive himself for the man he had once been.

I found this excruciating to witness and felt a huge sense of empathy for this man. What I wanted to tell him was this: none of us would ever wish to be judged by our darkest moments, and we each have to forgive ourselves for being trapped in pain and self-loathing because many of us were – and perhaps still are – just trying to survive. And for some of us, these negative behaviours developed when we were younger, as a means of coping with difficult circumstances.

One of the only ways we can move forward is by forgiving ourselves – by turning our faces towards the sun and not looking constantly over our shoulders.

Open your heart

The ability to be self-reflective and open your heart is a crucial aspect of spirituality. Many of us were raised in an environment where we were taught to be suspicious and mistrustful of others, and to compete with our peers for success. But our focus needs to be on accepting ourselves for who we are and recognizing that we are enough. When we nurture qualities of empathy, compassion and kindness towards others and ourselves, we come to understand that historically our fear-based thinking has only ever hindered our development, and we are now able to let it go.

Instead, we can cultivate greater empathy – that's the willingness and ability to imagine ourselves in another person's shoes, and to consider what life must be like for them. Empathy gives way to a more compassionate path of living, which is less judgemental and more tolerant, and is something that we can continue to hone and nurture. It allows us to bring a greater sense of fulfilment and happiness into our lives, which improves our relationships with others as well as with ourselves.

A spiritual awakening

How do we know when things are starting to shift? What does that feel like? When we undergo a spiritual awakening, we literally 'wake up' to life; we become fully conscious and open our hearts. We question our core beliefs, behaviours and the way that we were raised, and we begin to see that there is much more to life than what we may have previously understood there to be.

It can be an unsettling experience initially, because we can start to feel confused about the world and begin to question: *What is life all about?* We can feel disconnected from friends and family as we begin to recognize that we have established a false self in order to gain acceptance and approval. It can be a painful time when we come to realize that our unwell voice has been causing us endless pain and suffering, and that unconscious and dysfunctional patterns have been repeated within our family.

These are significant milestones that we need to acknowledge as we begin to connect to our higher self. It is important at this time to continue to focus on what brings us joy. Joy keeps us on the right path and allows the universe to deliver what we want. Joy is magnetic, and it aligns us fully and completely with the universe and our spiritual selves.

So make the choice today, right now, to do more of what brings you joy – whatever feels meaningful and good to you. The more you allow yourself to have those experiences, the more confident you'll be in the life that you are creating for yourself.

Embracing a connection to your spiritual self

The development of a spiritual practice is a subjective process. Often I speak to people who get frustrated when they aren't able to successfully subscribe to someone else's formula for spiritual enlightenment. But remember, those demons of comparison are totally unhelpful to you, and are rooted in the unwell voice. This is *your* journey, and you must try not to allow what others are doing to divert you from your path and make you doubt yourself. The whole nature of this kind of spirituality I'm talking about here is that it's about you and your relationship with the universe (rather than anybody else's). Simply developing your practice and learning to trust your intuition will mean that you will know what is (or isn't) the right path for you.

In this book I've touched on different methods and exercises that have been helpful to both me and those I've worked with, but I suggest that you try out different ways of dealing with this part of yourself and stick with what works best *for you*. Speak to others who have explored spirituality and find out what's helped for them; spend time in nature; sit in silence for ten minutes every day; rest with your hand over your heart and tell yourself that you are loved. Enjoy the practice of spiritual surrender; it will give you so much comfort and relief.

Essentially, by working on a spiritual practice, you are connecting with a loving energy. I don't know if we even need to be able to quantify that or fully make sense of what it is or where it comes from. Perhaps it is simply that love is an energy existing in the world – or maybe it's something greater that rests in the stars, or even something that runs through your veins and gives you life.

All I know is that I trust that this powerful loving force exists, and that is beyond explanation. It's a connection to something greater than myself, this force and this faith that I've found most intensely healing, and I really hope that you will too.

#HealHack

In my experience, the best place to connect with something greater than ourselves is in nature. I've heard the most sceptical people report a connection to something spiritual when they were in awe of something wonderful in nature. I nearly fell off my chair when my very alpha and atheist friend Rob described being in the presence of God when he stood on the mountains in Canada. Get outside and look up at the sky – breathe, and open your eyes and your heart.

Recovery Tool: Setting and Maintaining Boundaries

Boundaries are a *big* part of healing, protecting and sustaining a life where we honour and meet our own needs. So many of us never learned how to have healthy boundaries in childhood, because we learned very early on that we needed to compromise and ignore our own needs. We took on roles within our family dynamics that then became entrenched, and so we took those roles with us into adulthood and sought to re-create those dynamics. We became the rescuer/the victim/the partygoer/the underachiever/the aggressor/the controller . . .

We perhaps struggled to establish boundaries because early on:

- We became enmeshed with a parent who was overly involved in our relationships, aspirations and achievements.
- Another family member was continually in crisis and our needs became neglected or ignored.
- We became a caretaker for a family member, and confused their needs with our own.
- Our academic/career path was dictated and controlled by our caregivers.

There are many reasons related to unprocessed trauma why we may have struggled to find our voice and establish boundaries that met our needs, but we can begin to make those changes now as an empowered adult. However, the unwell voice can make it very difficult to establish and maintain boundaries, because we have been so used to neglecting our own needs.

To begin to listen to ourselves can feel very unfamiliar, but be mindful not to confuse that with something that isn't right for you. In my early recovery journey, setting and maintaining boundaries was one of the most challenging things that I was faced with. I had no clue what a boundary was, never mind how to maintain it.

I grew up in an environment where my needs were either ignored or called into question by those around me. I truly believed that it was my duty to put everyone else's needs before my own. I thought I had an obligation to try to 'fix' others, and that it was my responsibility to limit another person's suffering.

Setting boundaries allowed me to grow in such inexplicable ways. It was a tool to communicate to others what I expected and felt I deserved, and it allowed me to determine a set of principles by which I came to live. I learned that, in not setting boundaries, I had never been able to put myself first and had been committing myself to a life of resentment, anger, sadness and loneliness. It was challenging for me and everyone around me when I began to find my voice, but I did it and you can too.

I think it's tempting at this point to try to explain yourself to those around you, and to try to legitimize why your behaviours might be changing. Look out for that unwell voice seeking validation in places that you are unlikely to get it (particularly if you've never had it from those people). Keep your cards close to your chest, share your process only with those you trust to support you, and keep going. The people around you don't need to give you permission to do this work. You are reason enough to commit to developing a more compassionate and loving way of living.

How do you know if you have
an issue with boundaries?

Do you:

- Put other people's needs before your own?
- Feel as though you don't belong and that no one knows you?
- Feel as though you are ultimately undeserving of love or happiness?
- Believe that setting boundaries would threaten your relationships?

What are the benefits of establishing
and maintaining boundaries?

Healthy boundaries encourage:

- Open and honest communication in relationships.
- A sense of empowerment and independence.

- The ability to ask for what you want and need.
- Being able to take responsibility for your own happiness.
- Being able to say no.
- Feeling seen and heard.

Examples of boundaries

'I'll check my email when I get into the office, and I'll respond to you then.'

'I am available to support you on Wednesday morning, but I'm not available for the rest of the week.'

'I can stay for three hours.'

'I appreciate you're angry, but you can't stay if you keep shouting.'

'I'd like to think about that before making a commitment.'

'I have a commitment at that time, can we agree another date?'

Establish your boundaries

In your journal, write down five character traits that you value and which are important to you.

For example, you may value:

1. Honesty
2. Kindness
3. Intelligence
4. Humour
5. Compassion

Give yourself a moment to reflect on these qualities. Fostering qualities that you value within yourself will help strengthen a sense of respect for yourself, and in turn will help you to establish and maintain boundaries. Can you write a few sentences about how you might nurture these qualities in yourself?

For example:

- *I will be kind to myself by giving myself time to read at least three times a week.*
- *I will reflect on reactions I have to events, and give myself space to show up and be honest with myself about my triggers.*

Next, write down five examples of where you think you have struggled to establish and maintain a boundary. This is not an opportunity for your unwell voice to beat you up! This is a chance for you to reflect on where you could begin to assert and establish firmer boundaries that are in line with your own values. For example:

1. *I work all weekend without extra pay/acknowledgement from my boss.*
2. *I drop everything to provide ad hoc childcare for my sister.*
3. *I cancel plans with my friend to make sure I'm always available to my partner.*
4. *I can't say no.*
5. *I don't meditate during the day because I don't have any time for me.*

Now write down five examples of how you might be able to put boundaries in place right now. For example:

1. *I can let my boss know that I'm unavailable to work over the weekend but I'm happy to make some time on Friday to look at the project.*
2. *I tell my sister that I'm available to babysit, but only for three hours on Saturday.*
3. *I tell my partner that I'm not able to make a date because I have plans with a friend already, but would he like to reschedule?*
4. *I respond to that guy who asked me out and say that I'm not interested in dating him.*
5. *I do ten minutes' meditation every morning before I start my day because I'm important.*

Boundaries are the structures within which you can grow and work on everything that you've learned on this journey. They will help to keep you safe, give you confidence and let the world know how you feel you deserve to be treated by others.

The Time Is Now

As we come to a close, I think it's important to remind ourselves that change takes faith, time, patience and persistence. This book is a guide to support you as you move forward with the rest of your life. These chapters and tools are there for you to refer back to and to revisit whenever you think you might need them. Healing is such a transformative experience, and it's worth coming back to this book in a few months' time or even a year, revisiting the themes that we've worked through and seeing what new insights you may be able to gain. I know first-hand that I've had to repeat and reinforce positive ideas and changes for them to really resonate deeply.

This is a time for you to be gentle and kind to yourself, as becoming aware and finding yourself in an awakened state can be wonderful but also painful. Remember that the progress you make is a set of small changes that lead to bigger shifts, so don't feel that you always need to be reading or working on something. Learning to 'be', to play and to experience joy is also a big part of this journey.

If you are coming to terms with unprocessed trauma, then you will likely feel sad and need to grieve for a period – and this is totally normal. I remember coming to terms with the fact that I'd been sad for a lot of my life, and as painful as this was, it was also a big catalyst for change.

If you find yourself acting out old patterns, then please know this is also very much part of the process. Every stumble is an opportunity to reflect, learn and move on.

If you recognize that you've fallen back into old patterns or you feel fatigued by the process of healing, be kind to yourself and remember that you've been through a lot. When we're struggling or in pain we need kindness and compassion, and there are no exceptions to that rule.

I see you and I wrote this book for *you*. In my life, I've learned something about what it is to be human and what is needed to heal – and I wanted to share that with you. Acknowledging the parts of yourself you are most ashamed of is an act of compassion, humility and shows a willingness to embrace what it is to be alive. If you feel scared, that's okay. Now is your chance to find courage. Let go of who you thought you 'should' be, and shine a light on the darkest parts of your soul – because as my favourite band The National once said, 'Baby, we'll be fine, all we gotta do is be brave and be kind.'

Further Reading

Melody Beattie, *Codependent No More: How to Stop Controlling Others and Start Caring for Yourself* (Hazelden Publishing, 2018)

Brené Brown, *Daring Greatly: How the Courage to Be Vulnerable Transforms the Way We Live, Love, Parent, and Lead* (Penguin Life, 2015)

Glennon Doyle, *Untamed: Stop Pleasing, Start Living* (Vermilion, 2020)

David Richo, *How To Be an Adult in Relationships: The Five Keys to Mindful Loving* (Shambhala Publications, 2002)

Michael A. Singer, *The Untethered Soul: The Journey Beyond Yourself* (New Harbinger Publications, 2007)

Bessel van der Kolk, *The Body Keeps the Score: Mind, Brain and Body in the Transformation of Trauma* (Penguin Books, 2015)

Index